Seven Step
Moral Inte

Seven Steps to
Moral Intelligence

Based on Imam Ghazali's teachings

Musharraf Hussain

KUBE
PUBLISHING

First published by Kube Publishing Ltd,
Markfield Conference Centre
Ratby Lane, Markfield,
Leicestershire LE67 9SY
United Kingdom
Tel: +44 (0) 1530 249230
Fax: +44 (0) 1530 249656
Website: www.kubepublishing.com
Email: info@kubepublishing.com

The right of Musharraf Hussain to be
identified as the author of this work has been
asserted by him in accordance with the
Copyright, Designs and Patents Act, 1988.

Cataloguing-in-Publication Data
is available from the British Library

Designed, typeset and printed in India

ISBN 978-1-84774-009-0 paperback

Contents

Contents

Preface

Every Ramadan during the last ten days of *i'tikaf* (spiritual retreat), I busy myself with the study of classical Islamic books. In Ramadan 2000, while in *i'tikaf*, I studied *Disciplining of the Soul: Refining the Character and Curing the Sicknesses of the Heart* by Imam Ghazali (may God have mercy on him), and was impressed by it as a straightforward guide for people who seriously want to develop their morality and spirituality. The clear translation by Dr T. J. Winter made the task of studying it very easy. I personally benefited from this study and began to deliver a series of lessons based on it.

Seven Steps to Moral Intelligence is also inspired by another book of Ghazali's, *Minhaj al-'Abidin*, in which he takes the reader through seven steps of spiritual development. Character building is a long-term and ongoing process; this book lays firm foundations for this process. I have sought to make this book accessible and approachable and have written chapters explaining morality, the Prophet's ﷺ moral virtues, the Divine Qualities and finally the moral vices.

In *Disciplining the Soul*, Imam Ghazali describes the process of self-development and provides clear guidelines towards attaining moral intelligence. This is a process which has many steps but I have enumerated seven steps for the sake of clarity in Chapter Five, which is the central chapter in this guide. Moral intelligence may therefore be defined as the application of one's intelligence to acquiring the right knowledge and skills in order to develop and then perfect good character by opposing one's ego.

The acquisition of good character begins with *self-motivation* (Step One), then with *realising* the need for *self-improvement* (Step Two), followed by believing that *self-improvement* is *possible* (Step Three). Step Four is looking at one's own faults or *self-examination*. The underlying principle in the whole process of moral development is renouncing your worldly desires (Step Five) which requires *self-control*. Step Six is the *method of treatment*. Finally, Step Seven is reviewing one's progress and monitoring oneself. This guide ends with a final chapter on how Imam Ghazali applied these teachings in his own life, for he was not only a renowned scholar and teacher, but also a great role model.

Chapter **One**

The Meaning and Scope of Morality

Islamic morality is a code of conduct revealed by God (Allah) and lived by the Prophets, and, in particular, that which was shown by the final Prophet Muhammad ﷺ, who explained his purpose as having 'been sent to perfect morality'. Muslims regard prophetic morality as the overriding guide to individual behaviour that they must adopt in their daily lives. It is also a universal guide that all rational people can aspire to. A closer look at Islamic morality shows that it is a universal code that, without exception, other religions and traditions promote as well.

Imam Ghazali defines morality as 'a firmly established condition of the heart, from which acts proceed easily without any need for thinking.' So it's a mindset, an attitude, as though one is programmed to doing good; morality is therefore

> Moral Character is . . .
>
> *Knowing the good, desiring the good and doing the good is shown by good habits of mind, habits of the heart and habits of action.*
>
> Thomas Lickona, educational psychologist

not the action but the driving energy behind the action.

The Purpose of Morality

Morality is concerned with promoting peace and harmony between people and avoiding harm to others. Basically it's about what sort of person we should all want to be and how we should all live together.

Morality serves many purposes:

1. To be characterized by the Divine attributes and qualities. The Messenger ﷺ said, 'You should be characterised by the attributes of God Most High.'
2. To copy the beautiful character of the Messenger of God ﷺ, since 'his character was the teachings of the Qur'an' and he is the most beautiful of role models.
3. Morality serves the social function of ensuring the well-being of others, in particular the weak and vulnerable members of society.
4. For personal development, morality counters egoism (self-centeredness) and develops a spirit of self-sacrifice.

Without guidance and moral teachings, people will not change. They will be caught up in the mesh of their selfish desires, and become self-centred. Islam offers Divine reward and promises Paradise. Moral development helps a person to have self-mastery enabling

> **The Golden Rule in Islam**
>
> *You cannot be a believer until you love for your brother what you love for yourself.*
>
> Prophet Muhammad ﷺ

her or him to serve and contribute to the well-being of others. When a person is able to subordinate an impulse to a moral virtue, when he can control certain feelings, circumstances and conditions, then that is moral living. The moral person lives by moral virtues that have been internalised.

5. Morals are a means to salvation in the next life. Here I would like to highlight some of the objectives that lie behind the acquisition of moral virtues. These life skills help in achieving a goal or a combination of several goals such as:

    a. Self-awareness
    b. Reconciliation and achieving peace
    c. Communication skills
    d. Team building
    e. Diagnostic skills or understanding the needs or ideals of others
    f. Organisational skills
    g. Discipline in carrying out specific objectives

6. Imam Fakhruddin Razi (d. 604 AH), commenting on the verse, *On that day We shall call every community with their imam* (Bani Isra'il 17: 71), says, 'There is another possible meaning of "imam" and that is as follows: there are many moral virtues and vices. Everyone possesses one or the other. There are people who are overwhelmed by anger (i.e. they are angry); others [who are] full of hatred or jealousy. On the other hand, there are those who are forgiving, brave or generous. So these virtues or vices are like an imam for him on the Day of Judgement; reward or punishment will be as a result of these moral virtues or vices.'

Morality is the key to joy and happiness. Ask yourself these three questions with respect to each moral virtue and reflect on the answers. For example, take the case of generosity:

1. What is it like to experience generosity?
2. When was the last time I was generous?
3. How does it feel to be generous?

Some words that express inner joy and happiness after practising these virtues		
Exhilarated	Overjoyed	Lively
Vigorous	Animated	Elated
Energetic	Euphoric	Ecstatic
Alert	Joyful	Empowered
Loved	Dazzled	Enthused
Excited	Intoxicated	Passionate

What makes morality different?

How does morality differ from etiquette, from law, social obligations and spirituality?

Etiquette (*adab*) is manners and conventional rules of behaviour like eating with the right hand, the dress code and greeting each other in peace (*taslim*).

Law (*fiqh*) deals with rules: the do's (the obligatory, recommended and permitted) and the don'ts (offensive and forbidden). These laws cover all aspects of a Muslim's life, including worship, marriage and divorce, and business. A breach of the law carries penalties either in this worldly life or in the Hereafter – but that is not the case with morality. Although a breach of the moral code does not incur any legal penalty, it carries with it the significance of troubling the conscience and of incurring the greatest penalty of all – the Divine Wrath.

Social obligations like the rights of parents, relatives, children, neighbours, teachers, friends and animals (known as *huquq*) are also different from morality. The desire to meet the needs of others by supporting them, respecting them and fulfilling their rights is based on the deeply-held belief that all human beings have common parentage in Adam and Eve. This belief leads to the feelings of brotherhood and sisterhood whereby all humans are one family – 'the family of God'. All are equal and should have their human rights protected. Islam expects us to make the service of others part of the purpose of our lives.

The educationist Rosalind Hursthouse elaborates this human relationship as being 'willing to subjugate their egoistical desires in order to secure the advantages of co-operation. Like other social animals, our natural impulses are not solely directed towards our own pleasure and preservations but include altruistic and cooperative ones.'

Spirituality is defined as the awareness of the Lord of the universe, having faith in His Benevolence, trust in His infinite Power, and accepting the responsibility of being His representative on Earth as well as being His trusted servant.

> The Prophet ﷺ said,
>
> *The best amongst you is the one who benefits others the most.*
>
> (Tirmidhi)

Meaning and Scope

One Islamic term used to describe spirituality is *taqwa*, which means God-consciousness, piety, fear of God, and awareness of and attentiveness towards God. Another term for spirituality is *ikhlas*, which means having sincerity and genuineness towards God in one's intention and actions, and loving God as He is the One who truly deserves our love. The Islamic forms of worship like the five daily prayers (*salat*), remembrance (*dhikr*) and glorification (*tasbih*) of God, singing devotional poetry (*qasa'id* or *anashid*), invoking His beautiful Names (*al-asma' al-husna*) and fasting (*siyam*) are all effective spiritual exercises. The result of all these is drawing closer to God, feeling happy in His presence, recognising the Lord and living in His presence.

Spirituality is humankind's relationship with its Lord, whilst morality is people's relationship with each other as well as with all other living creatures. However we should understand that spirituality provides the motivational energy for living the moral life.

Religion and Morality

Islam is a whole way of life, constantly guiding and leading its followers towards Paradise and ultimate salvation. Morality is one of its important subjects. The Prophet ﷺ said 'religion is morality.' But this does not mean religion is *only* morality, rather its pre-eminence in Islam is being emphasised here. Morality is not a particular act but the desire to act righteously – it is a mindset.

Moral acts are a sign of the inner will.

Imam Ghazali

Ali Izetbegovic, the Bosnian writer and politician, explained the link between religion and morality, when he said, 'as a phenomenon of human life, morals cannot be rationally explained, and as such, in them lie the first and perhaps the only practical argument for religion.' This does not mean morality is irrational. To live a moral life is essentially to live a pure, good and happy life. The arguments for such a life are self-evident. *We can understand the self-evident nature of a moral life by considering the absurdity of living immorally.* Who would consider living a life of dishonesty, cruelty and deceit? Therefore moral values are the foundation of a happy and successful life and of a virtuous community and society.

What is a virtue or a character trait?

Ghazali said 'moral virtue is a firmly established condition.' In other words, it is a disposition well-entrenched in its possessor; as might be said, it is something that 'goes all the way down', unlike habits, such as tea-drinking. A disposition, far from being a single track propensity to be honest or even act for certain reasons, is multi-track. It is concerned with many other acts as well: with emotions and emotional reactions, choices, values, desires, perceptions, attitudes, interests, expectations and sensibilities.

For a person to possess a virtue is to have a certain complex mindset. And this explains the extreme recklessness of attributing

> *Character cannot be made except by a steady long continued process.*
>
> Phillips Brooks

a virtue to someone on the basis of a single act that he or she does.

Take a person whose dealings are honest and who does not cheat. If such acts are done simply because honesty is the best policy, or because of a fear of being caught out, rather than recognising that 'to do otherwise would be dishonest', then these are not the acts of an honest person. An honest person cannot be identified simply as one who, for example, always tells the truth, nor even as one who always tells the truth because it is the truth, for one can have the virtue of honesty without being tactless or indiscreet. Furthermore, to possess such a disposition fully is to have perfect virtue, which is rare. So possessing a virtue is a matter of degree between those who may be described as truly virtuous and those who lack it completely.

Moral character is a principle of human nature which is real, effective, purposeful and meaningful. Moral character is like a lighthouse, a permanent source of illumination and guidance. The moral principles that govern human growth and happiness are woven into the fabric of every civilised society. And these moral principles comprise the foundations of every sound family and viable social institution.

The reality of moral principles becomes obvious to anyone who thinks deeply and examines the cycles of social history. These principles appear time and time again, and the degree to which society recognises and lives in harmony with them moves it towards either unity and stability or disintegration and discord.

These moral principles are universal. All authentic religious traditions teach honesty, compassion, justice,

The Meaning and Scope of Morality

Value	Meaning	Benefits/Behaviour	Opposite
Honesty	To be truthful in word, action and intention	Integrity, sincerity and trustworthiness, probity and scrupulousness	Dishonesty
Compassion	To have pity on deserving people and help remove their difficulties	Respect, co-operation, friendship, pity, love and benevolence	Pitilessness
Justice	To give others what is due to them and ensure their rights are fulfilled	Trust and sense of equality, fraternity and respect	Cruelty
Courage	To withstand difficulties and to strive to achieve great works at risk to oneself	Self-reliance, responsibility, and freedom	Cowardice
Patience	To bear difficulties calmly without complaining; to avoid reacting hastily	Perseverance, fortitude and calmness in difficult times	Anger, Haste
Forgiveness	Surrendering one's right to get even with the offender	Co-operation and friendship	Revenge
Generosity	To give freely and voluntarily for the benefit of others	Friendship, loyalty, love, unselfishness, and cheerfulness	Miserliness
Humility	To recognize one's own inadequacies and weaknesses and to serve others without attracting attention or seeking approval	Gentleness, calmness and easygoingness, courtesy and politeness	Arrogance
Gratitude	To be thankful for the good that has been done		Ingratitude

courage, gentleness, forgiveness, humility, modesty, generosity and patience. They are indeed self-evident or obvious truths. The table (p. 9) describes ten moral values, their opposites and their consequences.

The figure below illustrates Imam Ghazali's three-point strategy for developing moral character.

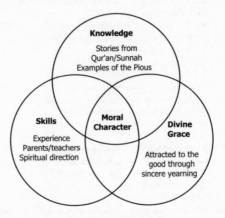

Knowledge
Stories from
Qur'an/Sunnah
Examples of the Pious

Skills
Experience
Parents/teachers
Spiritual direction

Moral Character

Divine Grace
Attracted to the
good through
sincere yearning

Neither human reason nor nature can provide in themselves the foundations for morality. For example, the principle of fairness within the family is not by itself going to foster good relations – a spouse might ask, 'If my spouse doesn't do his or her share of the work, then why should I do mine?' Instead, there has to be a spirit of generosity. Human selfishness cannot be the basis of morality since humanity is blinded by self-interest and desire. Humanity must seek to become selfless.

This is where religion is important as it acknowledges a source of grace and power outside of humanity that can provide a solid foundation for morality.

Religion provides that basis by guaranteeing Divine pleasure and reward in this world and salvation in the Hereafter. However, philosophers, religious or otherwise, also study morality. This study is called ethics.

Ethics is of two kinds:

1. *Descriptive Ethics* which describes moral rules and practices thus making familiar different moral ideas.
2. *Normative Ethics* which sets up a norm (or standard) by which moral principles are assessed.

For Muslims, the norm is set by the Majestic Qur'an and the Sunnah of the beloved Messenger of God ﷺ. It is from these two sources that Islamic morality derives its authority. Muslims believe in these sources unstintingly, and so they accept Islamic morality as a duty.

Islamic morality is normative, in contrast to 'moral relativism', where each person is his or her own authority and one person's opinion is as good as another's and there are no set standards. It is a free-for all, where everyone fights for their own interests. This might amount to the naked pursuit of self-interest.

However, Islam teaches that Muslims must strive to become what God calls them to become.

Understanding Moral Development

This is the development, growth and acquisition of universal moral virtues: honesty, compassion, patience, modesty, generosity, humility, justice, forgiveness and courage. It is the progress an individual makes to overcome self-interest and selfishness, preferring to

11

fulfil the needs of others rather than seeking self-gratification. Moral development is the internalization of these universal moral values and the conditioning of oneself to live by these values.

Moral development is the opposite of hedonism, where the self-centredness and narcissism of the self-focused individual remains busy in gratifying her or his own needs.

Imam Ghazali's teaching on moral development (see Chapter Five) offers a practical guide that sets out to give advice and tips in the context of real life situations. It is a didactic approach that encourages and spurs the person on to acquire these values. This is in sharp contrast to modern psychological approaches to moral development.

Professor Drew Westen, a professor of psychology at Harvard University, says that, 'Psychologists are more concerned with the roles of cognition (or the process of thinking, understanding and memorising) and emotion in the child's evolving sense of right and wrong.' They have several theories to explain the role of cognition in moral development. Cognitive-social theories hold that moral behaviours like other behaviours are learned through processes such as social conditioning and modelling. Morality develops as children discover by trial and error as well as through instruction that certain activities are rewarded and others punished. They anticipate the particular outcomes of their behaviours and they develop conditioned emotional responses to them as well.

The famous educationist Jean Piaget focuses more upon moral reasoning than moral development. This cognitive-developmental theory argues that moral development proceeds through a series of steps that reflect cognitive development. The theory of the educationist Lawrence Kohlberg shares basic ideas with Piaget's approach. He proposes a three-level theory of moral development:

1. Level One: *Pre-Conventional* – Morality centres on avoiding punishment and obtaining reward.
2. Level Two: *Conventional* – Morality centres on meeting moral standards learned from others, avoiding their disapproval and maintaining law and order.
3. Level Three: *Post-Conventional* – Morality centres on abstract and carefully considered principles.

At the pre-conventional level, the child follows moral rules simply for reward or to avoid punishment. At the conventional level, individuals define what is right by the standards they have learned from other people, particularly from respected authorities. People with conventional morality justify their choice of moral action on the basis of their desire to gain approval or to avoid disapproval of others. Post-conventional morality is based on abstract, self-defined principles that may or may not accord with the dominant morals of the time.

The logic of the theory is that at the pre-conventional level, the person accepts moral standards only in so far as doing so is personally advantageous – this is the ethic of hedonistic self-interest. At the conventional level, the individual believes in the normal rules that he has learned. At the post-conventional level, he sees values as absolute and Divine in origin if he is a believer. The theories of moral development discussed so far emphasise the role of cognitive judgement and decision-making in moral development. Other approaches, however, focus on the emotional side, prominent among these being the psychodynamic theories.

The psychodynamic view of moral development proposes that children start out as relatively narcissistic and self-interested, for example, when a child wants an extra piece of cake, he or she simply grabs it. This need-gratifying orientation begins to change with the development of the conscience between the ages of two and five. Moral development thus stems from identification, or internalisation: children take in the values of their parents, which are at first external and they then gradually make them internal by adopting them as their own. The motivations behind this adoption are sometimes guilt and sometimes empathy.

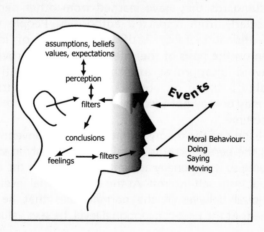

Moral Behaviour and the Thinking Process

This model attempts to explain the link between external events and moral behaviour. Beliefs affect the perceptions people have. Those perceptions then affect their conclusions, which produce feelings. These feelings then drive behaviour. Filters are cognitive processes that prevent us perceiving events accurately; they also prevent us from acting out our true desires. These defence mechanisms act as a further set of filters to protect us from psychological damage. They also prevent an accurate psychological reading of other people.

Assumptions are beliefs we hold about the way the world or other people or ourselves should or ought to be. Assumptions therefore make up our value system, but expectations and beliefs can be changed through good management and intent and actions. Values are deeply-held assumptions, and they are difficult to change, and that is why moral values learned in childhood will develop as the person grows older.

A List of Moral Virtues

Imam Ghazali, like other Muslim philosophers, accepted the Greek idea of the soul having three faculties and to each faculty he assigned a virtue. So the *rational* faculty develops wisdom, the *aggressive* (or irascible) faculty develops courage, whilst the *lustful* (or passionate) faculty develops temperance. When there is harmony between the three, they lead to the development of the virtue of justice. Ghazali uses the following verse of the Qur'an to support this idea:

The believers are those who believe in God and his Messenger, then have not doubted, and have struggled with their possessions and their selves in the way of God; those are the truthful ones. (al-Hujurat 49:15)

The Soul

Wisdom – Intelligence

Justice

Courage – Ethos

Temperance – Pathos

According to Ghazali, believing and being certain refers to wisdom. The struggle with possessions refers to temperance that is in turn associated with controlling the passions. The struggle with the self refers to the virtue of courage, associated with the management of the irascible soul.

Ghazali gives subdivisions for each of the four cardinal virtues. These are shown in the first table below. The second table shows the virtues according to the moral philosopher Ibn Miskawayh. The third table shows a comprehensive grouping of all the virtues based on other sources as well. Finally, a full list of virtues and vices, along with their meanings, is given.

Wisdom	Courage	Temperance	Justice
Sagacity	Generosity	Modesty	Political
Sound Judgment	Self-Assurance	Shyness	Moral
Discernment	Magnanimity	Forgiveness	Economic
Right Opinion	Endurance	Patience	
	Patience	Generosity	
	Nobility	Cheerfulness	
	Bravery	Self-Control	
	Composure	Orderliness	
		Contentedness	

The four cardinal virtues and their sub-divisions according to Imam Ghazali

It should be noted that Ghazali, unlike Ibn Miskawayh, does not give any subdivisions of justice because he regards this virtue 'as the foundation upon which heaven and the earth have been established.'

Wisdom	Courage	Temperance	Justice
Intelligence	Magnanimity	Modesty	Friendship
Retention	Fearlessness	Gentleness	Forgiveness
Prudence	Fortitude	Self-Control	Kindness
Lucidity	Steadfastness	Liberality	Reciprocity
Comprehension	Patience	Contentedness	Honesty
Sound Judgement	Endurance		Generosity
Ignorance	**Cowardice**	**Greed**	**Violence**

The four cardinal virtues, their sub-divisions and opposites according to Ibn Miskawayh (from Tahdhib al-Akhlaq)

17

Seven Steps to **Moral Intelligence**

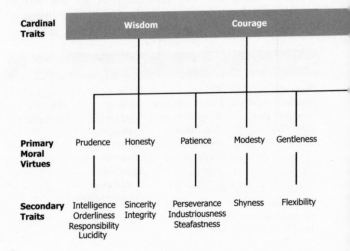

Cardinal Traits	Wisdom		Courage		
Primary Moral Virtues	Prudence	Honesty	Patience	Modesty	Gentleness
Secondary Traits	Intelligence Orderliness Responsibility Lucidity	Sincerity Integrity	Perseverance Industriousness Steafastness	Shyness	Flexibility

Personal and Social

Empathy Consideration Understanding	Self-Esteem Self-Confidence Assertiveness	Love Freedom Self-Discipline

The relationship between Cardinal, Primary and Secondary Moral Virtues, together

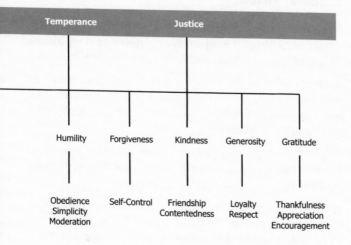

Temperance		Justice		
Humility	Forgiveness	Kindness	Generosity	Gratitude
Obedience Simplicity Moderation	Self-Control	Friendship Contentedness	Loyalty Respect	Thankfulness Appreciation Encouragement

Benefits and Outcomes

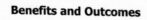

Rationality	Co-operation	Respect for Human
Diligence	Tolerance	Rights
	Sense of Unity	Accepting Diversity
		Social Obligation

with the interconnections of moral virtues and their personal and social benefits.

Cardinal Virtues

Wisdom: Having a wide range of knowledge and experience of life and judiciously applying it to daily affairs. This is being sagacious, prudent, lucid and optimistic.

Courage: The ability to overcome fear and to make an accurate judgment of risk-taking. The courageous person can face difficulties, overcome obstacles and struggle to achieve good deeds.

Temperance: Having self-discipline and the ability to control one's physical needs like sexual desire, hunger and thirst.

Justice: To be impartial in one's words, actions and decisions. A just person treats everyone fairly, irrespective of their background and ensures that people are given their due.

Primary Moral Virtues

Patience: To remain calm and composed in times of difficulty. A patient person will endure pain and grief in order to accomplish a particular task.

Modesty: To be shy by nature and to recognize the value of one's own privacy as well as that of others. A modest person lowers his or her gaze and dresses and acts modestly.

Gentleness: A gentle person is polite, courteous, and readily adapts his or her behaviour to the particular circumstance of each individual or situation without abandoning her or his principles of integrity.

Humility: To be humble and conscious of one's own failings and shortcomings. Humility leads a person to serve others without expecting praise from them.

Forgiveness: To forsake revenge when one is capable of retaliating. It is the willingness to stop feeling resentful about someone who has wronged you. It is surrendering the right to get even.

Gratitude: Being thankful, appreciative of others and acknowledging them openly and desiring to return the favour in a better way. Praising the goodness of others is a common mode of gratitude.

Kindness: To help and support those in need by having empathy and providing relief from suffering.

Honesty: To be truthful and genuine in words, deeds and thoughts. A person who is honest is sincere and trustworthy.

Generosity: To give cheerfully something that one values to someone who hasn't requested it, putting the needs of others above one's own. A generous person makes sacrifices for others that cost him or her personally.

These ten virtues are the primary building blocks of good character.

Observed Traits: Secondary Qualities and Life Skills

Orderliness: The ability to organize oneself meticulously in order to achieve a set goal. It's the ability to successfully plan and execute a project through one's own initiative.

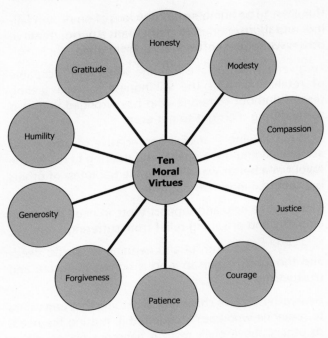

Responsibility: A sense of duty which urges one to fulfil that duty. A responsible person has a sense of being called to account for her or his actions, and has the ability to act independently.

Prudence: The ability to assess accurately the consequences and outcomes of complex issues. It is an essential facet of wisdom.

Lucidity: The ability to express oneself clearly and unambiguously in speech and writing.

Optimism: The ability to see the brighter side of difficult situations, and the inclination to be hopeful. Optimists have confidence in themselves, their colleagues, and above all a firm trust in God Almighty.

Perseverance: Being steadfast in pursuing a set goal. A persevering person will strive hard to achieve her or his goals despite facing difficulties internally and externally. Her or his resolve does not weaken.

Industriousness: The ability to work hard consistently and constantly and to put in long hours until the goal is achieved and the duty fulfilled.

Steadfastness: To be firm and unwavering in times of crisis. A steadfast person will not compromise his or her principles for immediate gain.

Shyness: Lowering of the gaze and being reserved in conduct and speech, avoiding obscenity and lewdness.

Flexibility: The ability to adapt to new situations when required without bending rules or principles.

Obedience: Carrying out orders given by those in authority, the first and foremost being God, then the Messenger ﷺ and then finally all those who are placed in authority over us. The authority of God and the Messenger is absolute whilst that of those in authority is conditional. The obedient person accepts these orders as his own decisions and carries them out diligently and faithfully so long as they do not contravene the fundamental principles and norms of religion.

Simplicity: The ability to avoid luxury and sophistication. A simple person dresses and acts in a natural way, consistent with her or his beliefs. This allows others to see and know the individual as he or she really is.

Moderation: Avoiding extremes of thought, action and behaviour. A moderate person strives to stick to the middle way in all things.

Self-Control: The ability to control one's desires, feelings and deeds. Having the self-mastery to avoid self-indulgent and selfish behaviour.

Friendship: The ability to build mutual affection and regard for people with whom one shares common concerns, issues, hobbies and interests. Being willing to serve and contribute to the welfare of others.

Contentedness: To be happy and satisfied with one's lot and purpose in life. A content person is grateful to God for her or his situation and status.

Sincerity: Being genuine in one's intentions, actions and behaviour. A sincere person ensures that his or her motives and behaviour are consistent, and that there is no discrepancy between how one is and how one seems to be.

Integrity: Moral probity. Living by and embodying moral virtues.

Loyalty: Being true and faithful to one's friends, relations, country, and so on. A loyal person shows allegiance and will defend and demonstrate his or her loyalty.

Respect: Holding others in esteem and regard according to their rights, status and circumstances. A respectful person will not cause any form of harm to others.

A List of Moral Vices

Arrogance

Imam Birgivi, a sixteenth-century Turkish scholar, defines arrogance as 'a state in which we are convinced that we have the right to be above others.' The following vices are different forms of arrogance:

Boasting: Praising one's own abilities, possessions, lineage and achievements with indulgent pride and satisfaction.

Bragging: Making boastful statements about oneself.

Contempt: Feeling that others are worthless, beneath due consideration and deserving of scorn.

Insolence: Being offensive and insulting others.

Disdain: Thinking of oneself as being superior to others and rejecting them.

Derision: Humiliating others by mocking them, making fun of them, lampooning them, caricaturing them and calling them names.

Ostentation: Displaying one's piety, achievements or wealth with the intention of impressing others.

Vanity: Desiring that others admire one's personal attainments or appearance.

Anger

Anger is a burst of uncontrolled passion aimed at someone who has hurt you or is threatening to hurt you. It is a vengeful attack with the aim of destroying or punishing a perceived enemy. Anger can take the following forms:

Belligerence: Seeking conflict and being aggressive towards others.

Vengeance: Inflicting punishment on someone who has harmed you.

Rancour and Hatred: Feeling enmity and hostility towards others without any legitimate reason and wishing harm upon others.

Malice: The intention to do evil to others.

Envy

Envy is the wish to see a person one dislikes becoming deprived of a blessing, although the loss of that blessing does not affect the envier in any way. Envy shows itself in different ways:

Resentment: Bitter feelings against someone who is envied.

Prejudice: Becoming intolerant of and discriminating against someone.

Despair: A sense of hopelessness in which one fears for his or her own well-being.

Greed

Greed is the excessive desire for wealth and worldly things and can take many forms:

Miserliness: Clinging to one's possessions and unwillingness to share with others. A disastrous outcome of this is that the miser is miserable: always in a wretched state of mind, constantly depressed and discontented.

Narcissism: The tendency to be self-centred and focused on gratifying one's own needs.

Gluttony: Excessive greed or the unbridled desire for more food and drink. It is commonly believed by spiritual people that too much food and drink harms the heart physically as well as spiritually. Fasting is the best antidote to this vice.

Moral Vices
The Thorns of Human Misery

KEY POINTS

- Morality aims to promote harmony between people and to avoid causing harm to others.

- Morality is the key to personal happiness and joy.

- Morality is a mindset or the desire to act righteously. It is related to but not the same as good manners (*adab*), rules (*fiqh*), social obligations (*huquq al-'ibad*) and spirituality (*tasawwuf*).

- Morality is concerned with developing virtues or good character traits. This includes not only behaviour but emotions, reactions, choices, desires, perceptions, attitudes, interests, expectations and sensibilities.

- Morality emerges from the interplay of knowledge and skills with the giving of Divine Grace.

- Moral development relies on fulfilling the needs of others and overcoming self-satisfaction.

- While assumptions about how the world, others and ourselves cannot be easily changed, our expectations and choices can be – and that is moral development.

- The four cardinal virtues are wisdom, courage, temperance and justice; the four cardinal vices are arrogance, anger, envy and greed.

Chapter Two

Moral Virtues of the Messenger ﷺ

The Prophet Muhammad ﷺ is seen as the most excellent role model for Muslims. His moral character was so wonderful that anyone who met him once would long to be with him again. His radiant face was lit with a broad smile and he was softly-spoken and eloquent. His company created a warm and loving atmosphere that pleased everyone. The Qur'an says: *By God's mercy, you were gentle with them. If you had been harsh and hard-hearted they would have left you.* (Al 'Imran 3:159)

Anas ؓ was eleven years old when the Prophet ﷺ arrived in Madinah. Anas used to spend most of his time with him. He recalled that 'I served the Messenger for ten years and he never once rebuked me or reprimanded me. He never said "why did you do it?" or "why didn't you do it?" ' (Bukhari)

'Ali ؓ reminisced about his loving company in these glowing words 'he

> *The Prophet ﷺ was so loving, kind, helpful and resourceful that when people called upon him, he would say – 'at your service'.*
>
> (Abu Nu'aym)

Moral Virtues

was the most generous, naturally lenient and most kind with those around him.'

In this chapter, we describe the moral characteristics of the Prophet ﷺ to show how he ﷺ lived a morally-rich life. The Qur'an indicates this when it says, *Surely your character is most sublime.* (al-Qalam 68:4)

When 'A'ishah ؓ was asked to describe his character, she simply said, 'he was a living Qur'an', that is, he lived by and acted on the teachings of the Qur'an.

The famous poet Imam Busiri describes beautifully the Prophet's character in his famous poem the *Burda* (meaning 'The Cloak'):

> Surpassing the prophets in beauty and character
> None may equal his wisdom and generosity
>
> If he is the Sun of Mercy, they, its stars,
> Come shining forth in times of darkness
>
> How beautiful he looks in manly form,
> Decorated with wonderful character
>
> Fresh as the rose petal, honourable as the full moon
> With oceanic generosity and leonine courage

The Honesty of the Messenger ﷺ

The Makkans used to call the Prophet 'the truthful' and 'the honest'. The Messenger ﷺ said, 'I am the honest one in the heaven and the honest one on the earth.' (Tirmidhi)

Even the Prophet's bitterest enemies admitted

> The Prophet's Purpose
>
> *I was sent to perfect moral character.*

to his truthfulness and honesty. Abu Jahl was asked of the Prophet ﷺ, 'Does he tell the truth or is he a liar?' He replied, 'By God, Muhammad is a truthful man and never lies.'

The Prophet ﷺ educated his followers to be truthful and honest. He taught that, 'Truth leads to goodness and goodness to Paradise. A person who always speaks the truth is truthful in God's sight. Likewise lying leads to evil and evil leads to hell. A person who always lies is a liar in God's sight.' (Bukhari)

The Prophet ﷺ was very scrupulous and nurtured this sense of honesty amongst the disciples.

The Justice of the Messenger ﷺ

This is one of the fundamental moral virtues. It means to be impartial in one's words, acts and decisions, and is about treating everyone fairly, irrespective of their background. Its importance can be understood from the fact that the Qur'an commands justice in several places, for example: *God commands justice and excellence.* (al-Nahl 16-90) The Qur'an is emphasising the fact that justice is an obligation upon everyone in all of their affairs. In another place it reiterates this point, *Indeed God commands you to deliver the trusts to their owners and whenever you make judgements between people then be just ....* (al-Nisa' 4:58)

The Prophet ﷺ said:

Leave doubtful things and do those that are certain. Indeed truth gives peace of mind whilst lies create doubts.

(Tirmidhi)

What leads to justice? It is the belief that all human beings are equal, the concept of human solidarity and fellow-feeling. The Messenger ﷺ preached this throughout his life.

The Prophet ﷺ was most just. A few days before his death, he came to the mosque where a crowd had gathered. He spoke to them saying 'O People! Is there anyone who I may have hurt? Here is my back, take your revenge. If I have been rude to anyone, my honour is here. Take your revenge. If I have confiscated anyone's wealth, then here is my wealth. Take what is yours. Don't think that I will be angry with you if you take your right. That is my way.' (Haykal)

The Compassion and Kindness of the Messenger ﷺ

Compassion is a moral virtue that consists of two elements: firstly to feel pity for another person, namely, to have sympathy and feel sorrow for his or her difficulty and secondly to take actions to remove the cause of that person's difficulty.

The moral virtue of compassion leads individuals to do acts that inspire and move those

The Prophet ﷺ on equality in Islam:

O people! Listen carefully. You Lord is one, an Arab has no superiority over a non-Arab, nor a non-Arab has any superiority over an Arab; also a white person has no superiority over a black one nor has a black person any superiority over a white one except in piety and good action.

(Bukhari)

who witness them. We will illustrate this here by reference to some wonderful examples of compassion from the life of the Prophet ﷺ.

The Prophet's compassion for people showed itself in different ways. For example he always wanted to make things easy for his followers. 'A'ishah ﷺ says 'whenever the Prophet had a choice between two things, he would always choose the easier option.' (Bukhari) He once said, 'If I had not been compassionate to my community I would have made obligatory the use of a tooth-stick in ritual purification (*wudu*).' (Bukhari)

One day he shortened the congregational prayer so much so that a companion asked him why he had shortened it. He said 'I heard a child crying and since women were praying behind me I wanted to quickly finish so that the mother could take the child.' (Muslim)

On the occasion of victory of Makkah, when the Muslim army was marching towards the city, the Prophet saw a dog on the roadside. She had just given birth to a litter of puppies; she was scared and growling. The Prophet ordered a Companion to stay by with her so that no one would harm her. (al-Shami)

> The Prophet's compassion and mercy as described in the Qur'an:
>
> *Grievous to him is that you suffer, he is ever anxious for your welfare, compassionate and merciful to the believers.*
>
> (al-Tawbah 9:129)
>
> *We only sent you as a mercy for the entire universe.*
>
> (al-Anbiya' 21:107)

The Forgiveness of the Messenger ﷺ

Forgiveness is a moral virtue that helps to build peace and reconciliation. Forgiveness is to forsake revenge when one is capable of exacting revenge.

The examples that follow illustrate beautifully how the Prophet ﷺ forgave even his bitterest enemies. God said to the Messenger ﷺ, *Forgive, enjoin the good, and turn away from the ignorant.* (al-A'raf 7:199)

The Prophet ﷺ asked Jibril السلام عليه to explain the meaning of this. He said 'God tells you to befriend those who break off from you, give to those who refuse to give to you and forgive those who are unjust to you.'

In the battle of Uhud, the Prophet's tooth was broken and his face was badly cut. The Companions were very saddened and angered by this and appealed to the Prophet to curse the Makkans who had done this. He replied, 'I was not sent to curse but sent as a summoner and a mercy. O God, guide my people for they do not know.' (Haykal)

One of the most moving incidents in the Prophet's life was his trip to the town of Ta'if that was near to Makkah. After he became disillusioned with the Makkans, the Prophet thought about preaching his message to the people of Ta'if. However, it turned out to be an extremely humiliating experience. Not only

> Forgiveness is. . .
>
> *The willingness to cease to feel resentment against an offender. It is surrendering the right to get even.*
>
> Michael Henderson, specialist in conflict resolution

did they refuse to listen to him, but they threw him out of town. They set the street-urchins, vagabonds and children upon him, who threw stones at him.

He was badly injured, so much so that his sandals were filled with blood. He took refuge in an orchard outside of Ta'if. He looked up at the cloud and saw Jibril عليه السلام who said, 'God has heard what people said to you and how they rejected you. He has sent the angel of the mountains to you.' The angel gave salutations of peace to the Prophet ﷺ and said, 'I am at your service. If you wish, I will cause the two mountains of Akhshabayn to crush the people of Ta'if.' The Prophet ﷺ replied, 'I wish that God will bring forth from them generations who will worship Him alone and associate none with Him.' (Bukhari)

Similarly, the Prophet's forgiveness of the Makkans after the victory of Makkah must be classed as one of the most remarkable examples of forgiveness in the annals of history. On that historic day, the Makkan public and leaders were all gathered in the Ka'bah, standing as prisoners anxiously waiting their fate. For nearly twenty years they had persecuted him, planned his assassination, and murdered his uncle and many close friends. They feared that they would be all wiped out. The Prophet ﷺ stood up, after praising God, and asked them, 'What do you think I will do with you?' They replied as one, 'You are a generous brother and generous nephew.' The Prophet ﷺ smiled and said, 'I say to you what my brother Yusuf said, "There is no blame on you: go, you are all free."' (Haykal)

Anas ﷺ reports that, 'The next morning at dawn, eight Makkan men came with the intention of killing the Prophet ﷺ. They were seized. However, the Prophet ﷺ

ordered that they should be freed. The Qur'anic verse was revealed to record this incident, *He is the one who restrained their hands from you*. (al-Fath 48:24)' (Muslim)

There was a sinister magician by the name of Labid ibn al-A'zam. He once performed magic on the Prophet ﷺ that had dire effects upon his health. The spell was eventually broken after the revelation of Surah al-Falaq and Surah al-Nas. Labid was exposed, but the Prophet ﷺ neither chided nor punished him. (Haykal)

The Muslim army was returning from an expedition lead by the Prophet ﷺ. It was noon and the scorching sun forced them to stop and rest. Everyone found a place for themselves. The Prophet ﷺ also took a nap under a tree. An enemy soldier by the name of Ghawrith ibn Harris was watching and, taking advantage of this situation, took out his sword and approached the Prophet ﷺ stealthily. The Prophet ﷺ opened his eyes and saw the danger. Ghawrith said, 'Who will save you from me?' Without any fear, the Prophet ﷺ replied with full faith, 'My Lord will save me!' Upon hearing this, Ghawrith began to tremble and the sword fell from his hands. The Prophet ﷺ quickly picked up the sword and said, 'Now tell me, who will save you from me?' He remorsefully said,

'A'ishah ﷺ succinctly sums up the Prophet's forgiving and clement nature: *'I never saw the Messenger ﷺ ever take revenge for an injustice done to him, he never struck anyone with his hands except in the battlefield, and never did he hit a servant or a woman.'*

(Bukhari)

'Become the one who is good to his captives.' The Prophet ﷺ forgave him and let him go. (Bukhari)

Anas ؓ reported that, 'One day I was walking with the Messenger ﷺ. He was wearing a Najarani cloak with a thick border. A Bedouin grabbed it and pulled it so forcefully that it left a mark on his neck. Then he said, "O Muhammad! Tell them to give me the money which you have," so he looked at him and smiled and ordered that he should be given something.' (Bukhari)

The Patience of the Messenger ﷺ

To have patience means to remain calm and composed in times of difficulty. This moral virtue manifests in different ways: waiting for one's turn, getting up early in the morning for prayer, taking the time to walk to the mosque for prayer, fasting and avoiding worldly pleasures, and so on.

Below, we will read how the best of God's creation nurtured patience in his disciples.

The Qur'an makes dozens of references to patience, for example:

O believers! Be truly patient. (Al 'Imran 3:200)

And indeed we will try you with fear, hunger, damage to your wealth and lives and give glad tidings to the patient. (al-Baqarah 2:155)

> The Messenger ﷺ once said, *'The affairs of a believer are most strange: they are all good. This is only for the believer. In good times he is grateful to God and in difficult times he is patient.'*
>
> (Muslim)

Anas ﷺ reports that the Messenger ﷺ passed by a woman who was crying near a grave. The Messenger ﷺ told her, 'Fear God and be patient.' She retorted, 'Be off, for you have not been affected like me.' She did not recognise him ﷺ. Someone told her that he was the Messenger of God ﷺ, so she went to the Messenger's apartment to apologise. She said, 'I didn't recognise you.' He told her that 'Patience is when you are first struck by affliction.' (Muslim)

Anas ﷺ reported that 'I heard the Messenger ﷺ say that God says "When I test my servant by taking from him his beloved and he is patient, I will reward both of them with Paradise."' (Muslim)

Ibn Mas'ud ﷺ said, 'I visited the Messenger ﷺ when he was ill with fever. I said, "You have high fever." He said, "Yes, my fever is equal to two men's fever." I said, "Then will you get double the reward?" He said, "Yes, when a believer is injured or pricked by a thorn, he is rewarded, his sins are erased and they fall off him like the leaves fall off a tree."' (Bukhari)

Abu Hurayrah ﷺ said, 'When God wants good for someone, He afflicts him with difficulties.' (Bukhari)

The Humility of the Messenger ﷺ

Humility means to be humble and conscious of one's own failings and shortcomings. It also has the notion of being simple and unpretentious,

> Abu Hurayrah ﷺ said, *'The Messenger ﷺ said, "The strong one is not a good wrestler, but one who can control his anger."'*
>
> (Bukhari)

and having no expectation of praise from other people for one's good works.

The Prophet Muhammad ☪ was a beautiful example of humility. Despite his most lofty station in the Divine scheme of things, he ☪ was extremely humble.

He ☪ was given the choice of being a 'Prophet-king' or a 'Prophet-slave'. He ☪ chose to be a 'Prophet-slave'. The angel Israfil said to him, 'God has been very generous to you because of your humility. You are the master of the children of Adam, on the Day of Judgement, [you will be] the first for whom the earth will open and the first who will intercede.' (Abu Nu'aym)

In poetic praise, Mawlana Ahmad Raza Khan wrote, 'Blessed be his ☪ unpretentious style and easygoing yet encouraging smile.'

He ☪ did not hesitate to carry out menial jobs and domestic chores like cleaning up, milking the goats and patching worn-out clothes. He happily rode on a donkey and would invite children to sit behind him. He visited the sick and the poor. He would sit anywhere in a gathering and mix with his Companions.

When the Muslims conquered Makkah without a fight, the Prophet ☪ entered the city in the most humble manner. He was sitting on his she-camel with his head bowed in humility so much so that his head touched the saddle.

> **The Prophet's Humility**
>
> *A man came to the Prophet ☪ and began to tremble out of awe. The Prophet told him, 'Relax, I am not a king. I am the son of a Qurayshi woman who eats dried meat.'*

When someone called out to him, 'O Best of Creation!', he replied, 'That is Ibrahim.' (al-Bayhaqi)

As the poet Busiri says:

> Blessed be his ﷺ awesomeness and dignity,
> Best was he in piety and humility.

The Generosity of the Messenger ﷺ

Generosity is to give away cheerfully something that one values to someone who has not asked for it. It is the opposite of miserliness.

Qadi 'Iyad says, 'The Prophet ﷺ had no equal in this noble quality . . . all who saw him described him so.'

Whenever people made a demand of the Prophet ﷺ, he would give his time, money or whatever else he could give.

The young Anas ؓ says, 'Once a Bedouin asked for financial help, and the Messenger ﷺ gave him a flock of sheep that was grazing in the valley. The man returned with the flock to his people and invited them to become Muslims: "Muhammad gives a gift to a man who does not fear poverty."' (Muslim)

> Blessed be our valued Patron,
> Who leads us out of adversity

Once a man came to the Messenger ﷺ and asked for support. The Messenger ﷺ told him, 'I do not have anything at the moment, but go and buy whatever you need

> **The Prophet's Generosity**
>
> *Jabir ibn 'Abdullah ؓ says, 'The Messenger ﷺ was not asked for anything to which he said no.'*

on my account and I will pay for it later.' 'Umar ؓ
remarked, 'You are not obliged to give anything, O
Messenger!'

Another man standing by said, 'O Messenger! Spend
and do not fear reduction from the Master of the
Throne.' The Prophet ﷺ smiled and pleasure could be
seen on his face. He ﷺ said, 'I am commanded to do
this.' (Tirmidhi)

> Blessed be that embodiment of grace,
> To whom heavenly birds sing praise

A disciple by the name of Mu'awwidh once presented
a dish of fresh dates and cucumber to the Messenger ﷺ
and in return he gave him a handful of gold coins.

> Blessed be the Prophet ﷺ, most distinguished,
> Matchless, exquisite and peerless.

Abu Hurayrah ؓ tells of a man from whom the
Messenger ﷺ had borrowed 250 kilogrammes (half a
wasq) of dates. The Messenger ﷺ returned to him a full
wasq and said, 'Half of it is repayment and the other
half a gift from me.'

Sahl ibn Sa'd ؓ tells a moving story, 'A lady came to
the Messenger ﷺ and presented a gift of sheet cloth
with a beautiful border around it and insisted that he
wear it. The Messenger ﷺ accepted it and wore it. He
came to the mosque and there was one Bedouin who
came up to him and said, "O Messenger! This is beautiful, can I have it?" The Messenger ﷺ took it off, folded
it and handed it to the Bedouin.' (Bukhari)

The Messenger ﷺ was most generous and magnani-
mous. He ﷺ said to 'Umar ؓ, 'If I had as much gold as

the mountains of Tihama, I would distribute it amongst you.' (al-Shami)

The generosity of the Messenger ﷺ was not to gain fame or win titles but to work for God's pleasure. Sometimes he distributed his wealth amongst the needy, sometimes to equip the needy, and at other times to attract people to Islam.

The Courage and Bravery of the Messenger ﷺ

Courage is the ability to face danger and fear. It is the opposite of cowardice.

Qadi 'Iyad, the Maliki jurist, says, 'The Prophet was often to be found in dangerous situations. More than once, he went into difficult places from which the valiant and heroic had fled. He was firm and did not leave. He advanced and neither retreated nor wavered.' (al-Shifa')

During the Battle of Badr, the Prophet ﷺ was in the thick of the fight and his valour was evident. Similarly in the Battle of Hunayn when the Muslim soldiers were fleeing and scattered, the Prophet ﷺ galloped on his mule towards the enemy and summoned the Muslims to fight.

> Blessed be his denunciation of rage
> Praised be his ﷺ chivalry and courage

One night there was a lot of commotion outside Madinah. People were frightened and came out of their homes. Some men mounted their horses and went to investigate. They

> **The Prophet's Courage**
>
> *Ibn 'Umar ؓ said, 'I never saw anyone more courageous, intrepid, generous or pleasing than the Messenger of God.'* (al-Darimi)

were surprised to meet the Prophet ﷺ coming back. He ﷺ explained to them that it was Abu Talha's horse that had gone on a rampage. (Haykal) This shows his courage to take risks in frightening and dangerous situations.

His ﷺ courage and boldness cannot be underestimated as he stood against the arrogant, ignorant and proud Makkans. He ﷺ did not make a single compromise on his principles. He ﷺ challenged the 'idolaters', he ﷺ stood up against the oppressors and stood by the oppressed.

> Blessed be Mustafa's ﷺ bravery
> Whose ﷺ jangling swords bore his testimony

The Modesty of the Messenger ﷺ

Modesty is the quality that makes a person shy. Such a person does not stare at people's faces and their eyes when seeing something offensive or disagreeable. This moral value stops a person from boasting, showing off and being vain.

Modesty with regards to God means to be shy of disobeying Him so that 'He does not find you in a place that He has forbidden you from nor does He find you absent from where He wants you to be.'

Abu Sa'id al-Khudri, a famous disciple of the Prophet, vividly described the Prophet's modesty when he said, 'He was

> The Messenger ﷺ said 'Modesty is part of faith, and modesty is absolutely wonderful' and 'when you are no longer modest you can do whatever you like.'
>
> (Bukhari)

43

more modest than a secluded virgin. When he disliked something we could see it in his face.' (Abu Dawud)

Aman reports that 'A man came to the Messenger ﷺ with traces of saffron on him. The Prophet did not say anything to him since he never confronted anyone with something they would dislike. When he left, he said, "Could you tell him to remove it?" ' (Abu Dawud)

> Blessed be his eyes, those gems
> From which Mercy's fountain stems
> Blessed be the look of affection
> Caring, kind, marked with compassion

The Gentleness of the Messenger ﷺ

Qadi 'Iyad defines gentleness (*hilm*) as 'a state of digni-fied bearing, and remaining calm despite provocation.' It is similar to patience, but not the same. The Messenger ﷺ was the most excellent example of gentleness.

Anas ؓ says, the Messenger ﷺ said, 'Make things easy and don't make them diffi-cult. Give glad tidings and don't create conflict.' (Bukhari and Muslim) Abu Hurayrah ؓ says a man asked for advice and the Messenger ﷺ said, 'Don't be angry,' and repeated this a few times. (Bukhari)

'Abdullah ibn 'Abbas related that the Messenger ﷺ said to Ashajj 'Abdu'l-Qays,

> The Messenger ﷺ on Gentleness
>
> *God is gentle and loves gentleness.*
>
> (Bukhari)
>
> *Whoever is deprived of gentleness is deprived of all goodness.*
>
> (Muslim)

'You have two wonderful qualities which God loves, gentleness and taking it easy.' (Muslim)

The Gratitude of the Messenger ﷺ

Hassan ibn Thabit was a renowned poet. When he became Muslim, he praised the Messenger ﷺ with his eloquent tongue, and one day he composed the following verse:

> My eyes have not seen
> Anyone more beautiful than you
> No woman ever gave birth
> To one like you
> You, formed without blemish,
> Were made
> As you wished to be created

The Messenger ﷺ was so moved by this eulogy that he ﷺ gave the poet his cloak and sat Hassan upon the pulpit. This is gratitude: receiving praise from others with thanks, an example of selfless action and acknowledgement of the kindness offered.

The Messenger ﷺ once said of Abu Bakr's ﷺ service: 'There is no one whose favour I have not repaid except for Abu Bakr's. God will reward him on the Day of Judgement. No one's wealth has benefited me more than that of Abu Bakr's. If I were to choose a friend it would be Abu Bakr. Beware, for your master is God's friend.' (Bukhari)

This is the greatness of mind that acknowledges every good deed. The Messenger ﷺ was very appreciative of his Companions' efforts and would praise them at every opportunity. Once he ﷺ said to Abu Bakr, 'You were my Companion in the cave and you will again be my Companion at the Fountain of Paradise.' (Bukhari)

To show the Messenger's acknowledgement of the great work of his Companions, Muhammad ﷺ conferred rich titles upon them. For example, he called Abu Bakr ﷺ, 'al-Siddiq' (The Truthful), 'Umar ﷺ, 'al-Faruq' (The Criterion of Truth), 'Uthman ﷺ, 'al-Ghani' (The Benevolent), 'Ali ﷺ, 'Bab al-'Ilm' (The Gate of Knowledge), Ibn 'Abbas ﷺ, 'Habr al-Ummah' (Scholar of the Ummah), and Khalid Ibn Walid ﷺ, 'Sayf Allah' (The Sword of God).

However, there are reports in which the Messenger ﷺ 'disliked praising others in front of them.' Imam Nawawi has reconciled these reports as follows:

'If the one who is praised has strong faith, is well disciplined and has sound judgment and there is no fear of spoiling him with praise, in that case there is no harm lavishing praise on someone. However, if there is a danger that praise will make him big-headed then one should refrain from praising him.' (Riyad al-Salihin)

Moral Virtues

KEY POINTS

- The Prophet was sent to perfect moral character and was described as 'a living Qur'an'.

- His worst enemies described him as 'trustworthy' (*al-amin*).

- He gave justice to all, regardless of creed, colour or social station.

- He was kind and compassionate, always helping the disadvantaged and the weak.

- He forgave his bitterest enemies, those who had tortured and ridiculed him, his family and his disciples.

- Even in the greatest trials, he remained patient and calm in adversity.

- In his humility, he saw himself as a slave of the All-Merciful, not as a king.

- In his generosity, he never refused any request for help.

- In his courage, he always faced great dangers valiantly.

- His modesty was like that of a secluded virgin.

- He always responded to harshness with kindness.

- He thanked God for his blessings and thanked others for their service and self-sacrifice.

Chapter Three

The Divine Attributes

How can the Divine Attributes mould human character?

The beautiful names of God describe His qualities. Just as He is peerless and unique in His being, so He is unique in His qualities. None is like Him. The Qur'an teaches us that God is to be addressed by these wonderful qualities of Compassion, Forgiveness, Justice, Gentleness, Gratitude, Generosity, Truth and Patience. God is Perfect, Holy and Most Sublime. These beautiful Names give us some glimpses of Divine Moral Characteristics.

As the Names represent the Divine moral character, the scholars have encouraged us to

> Moulding Human Character by the Divine Attributes
>
> The Messenger ﷺ said, *'You must be characterised by the characteristics of God Most High'*, and he ﷺ also said, *'God is characterised by ninety nine Names, whosoever is characterised by one of them enters Paradise.'*
>
> (al-Haythami)

'acquire the Divine Moral Virtues' or *takhalluq bi akhlaq Allah*. They recommend reciting the Names as litanies, that is, rehearsing them repeatedly so that one becomes familiar with each beautiful Name and aspires to live by it.

Imam Ghazali explains how the perfection and happiness of humanity consists in conforming to the Divine Attributes and in being moulded by the moral qualities of God. There are two ways for a person to acquire the Divine Qualities.

The first way is to have a proper and thorough knowledge of the meaning of the Divine Attributes. This requires understanding the realities of these attributes just as one understands her or his own characteristics.

The second way of sharing in their meanings is to become completely immersed in these Attributes like the angels. One's heart is filled with love for the Attributes and there is a yearning to assimilate them.

The Divine Attributes can be divided into two groups. The first group describes His Names of Beauty and Perfection

---

Reflection of the Divine Attributes

Know that the world of created beings is like clear water, reflecting the Attributes of God. Their knowledge, justice, kindness and patience reflect God's – like a heavenly star is reflected in running water. The water flowing in the stream changes many times, but the reflection of the moon and the stars in the water remains the same.

Mawlana Rumi, *Mathnawi*

(*asma' al-jamal*) and the second group describes His Names of Majesty (*asma' al-jalal*). Below I have compiled some Attributes from each group.

Group One – The Names of Divine Beauty and Perfection

Al-Rahman (The Compassionate), Al-Rahim
(The Most Merciful)
Al-Ghafur (The Forgiver), Al-'Adl (The Just)
Al-Latif (The Benevolent), Al-Halim (The Gentle)
Al-Shakur (Most Grateful), Al-Karim (The Generous)
Al-Sabur (The Patient), Al-Wadud (The Loving)

Group Two – The Names of Divine Majesty and Power

Malik al-Mulk (The King of Absolute Sovereignty)
Dhu'l-Jalal wa'l-Ikram (The Lord of Majesty
and Generosity)
Al-Darr (The Punisher), Al-Muntaqim (The Avenger)
Al-Qayyum (Self-Existing), Al-Qadir
(The All-Powerful)
Al-Qawi (The Strong), Al-Ba'ith (The Raiser of the Dead)
Al-Jalil (The Majestic), Al-Kabir (The Great)
Al-Mumit (The Slayer), Al-Jabbar (The Compeller)
Al-Qahhar (The Dominant), Al-Mutakkabir
(The Proud)

In this chapter, we will look at the Divine Moral Qualities from the first group and how we can develop them in ourselves:

Al-Rahman (Compassionate), Al-Ghafur (Forgiving), Al-'Adl (The Most Just), Al-Halim (The Gentle), Al-Shakur (The Most Thankful), Al-Karim (The Most Generous) and Al-Sabur (The Patient)

The Compassionate (Al-Rahman, Al-Rahim)

Al-Rahman and al-Rahim, the Compassionate, the Most Merciful, are derived from the Arabic root, *r-h-m*.

The Divine Mercy is both general and specific. It is general for all creation, believers and non-believers alike, whilst specific mercy is given to the believers. This is why the name al-Rahman is unique to God, whereas al-Rahim can be used by others. The Messenger ﷺ is also called Rahim: [*The Messenger* ﷺ] *is ever desirous of the believers, kind and merciful* (*rahim*). (al-Tawbah 9:128) Al-Rahman is sometimes used instead of the name of Allah: *The servants of the Most Merciful walk humbly on the earth.* (al-Furqan 25: 63)

The Divine Mercy envelopes everything and manifests itself in numerous ways, for example, in the act of creating the world, humanity, providing sustenance, blessing humanity with reason and intellect, giving humanity faith and so on. His supreme Mercy will be shown when He enters believers into Paradise and honours them with direct vision of His Countenance.

> The reward of mercy to others
>
> The Messenger ﷺ said, '*Be merciful to those on earth so that the One in Heaven will be merciful to you.*'
>
> (Bukhari)

The Forgiving (Al-Ghafur)

God is Ghafir, Ghaffar and Ghafur. These are derivatives of the Arabic verb, *gh-f-r*, which means to hide or cover something up. So al-Ghafir is the One who hides human sins, that is, He forgives them. Whilst al-Ghaffar is superlative in the highest degree, al-Ghafur is the exaggerated form, meaning the Most Forgiving. It is one of the most commonly repeated Divine Names in the Qur'an. Without His forgiveness no one can escape punishment.

So the forgiving Lord covers up and hides our sins on this earth and will forgive them in the hereafter. Our share of this beautiful Name is that we should cover up others' sins and not expose them.

Another way that God conceals our sins is by changing evil deeds into good deeds for those who repent, have faith and do good works (al-Furqan 25:70).

Every human being has both beauty and ugliness in herself or himself, so by ignoring what is ugly and mentioning what is beautiful or good, one shares in this Divine Attribute.

The Most Just (Al-'Adl)

The Divine Names al-'Adl and al-Muqsit express Divine Justice. He cannot be unfair or cruel to His creation in His acts or commands. He abundantly rewards those

> The Messenger ﷺ said, 'Whoever covers up the faults of a believer, God will cover up his faults in the Hereafter and whoever exposes the sins of a believer, God will expose him.'
>
> (Tirmidhi)

Divine Attributes

who do good and justly punishes those who commit sins.

The righteous will be in Paradise, and the wicked will burn in Hellfire. (al-Infitar 82:13-14)

The first lesson from this Divine Name is that we believe in His Justice and do not question His acts or commands, even if they seem to be against us: *You may dislike something although it is good for you, or like something although it is bad for you, God knows and you do not.* (al-Baqarah 2:216)

As humanity is unaware of the Divine plan and is not able to avert it, we should simply accept that the Best of Planners has the most care and regard for us. The second lesson learnt is that a person should be fair and just in all his or her dealings with fellow human beings.

The Gentle (Al-Halim)

God is Gentle because He does not quickly reprimand sinners and rebellious people. He neither loses His temper nor treats people harshly. Despite having the power of revenge, He gives respite. If He were ever to punish humanity in full for their sins, none would remain alive. In the Qur'an, numerous examples of God's grace are given, about how He has blessed humanity with so much that they can not keep an account of these blessings. The Qur'an says: *If God was to hold people accountable for their injustices then not a single living creature would remain. But He gives respite for a fixed period.* (al-Nahl 16:61)

People deny God. They insult Him. They rebel against His Divine commandments and they associate partners with Him, but He continues to have mercy upon them and look after them. He remains undisturbed by their provocations.

As we recite this beautiful Name let us learn to be gentle and forgiving and not be quick to chase after other people for their faults.

So gentleness (*hilm*) is an active quality of the soul that enables a person to control his or her fierce temper. The Prophet Abraham عليه السلام is described in the Qur'an as 'gentle', for instance, he would eat only when a guest had arrived. One day, when two men arrived, he immediately had a ram roasted for them. However, they turned out to be the angels who had been sent to destroy the people of Lot. He began to plead to God to forgive the people of Lot and not punish them.

The Most Thankful (Al-Shakur)

God is the Most Thankful and appreciative. He acknowledges the tiniest good deeds of humanity and greatly rewards them. His appreciation of good acts takes many forms: He praises the righteous people, rewards them, blesses them with favours or removes obstacles from their lives. In short God is al-Shakur or the Most Thankful.

In a tradition, this thankful nature of God is clearly illustrated. The Messenger ﷺ said, 'A traveller was passing through an oasis when he came to a well, and he climbed down it and drank to his heart's content. When he came out of the well he saw a thirsty dog licking the wet sand. The man went down again and filled his moccasin with water and gave the dog the water to drink. God thanked the man.' (Bukhari)

God rewards our small deeds abundantly, sometimes ten times, sometimes seven hundred times and yet at other times without bounds and limits. This is our thankful Lord.

We also need to be thankful to Him. The Qur'an says: *If you are thankful I will increase you and if you are ungrateful, then my punishment is severe.* (Ibrahim 14:7)

So we should thank anyone who is good to us, praise him or her and if possible reward her or him by giving a better gift of kindness in future.

The Most Generous (Al-Karim)

The Most Generous gives without being asked and gives abundantly beyond one's expectations. He gives beyond measure. Whoever seeks His refuge is granted it and people can appeal to Him directly without mediators. This is our Generous Lord, al-Karim. God gives without expecting anything back. He has no motive of or need for recompense.

Our work, struggle, devotion and sacrifice should all be for the sake of Divine pleasure and not only for getting into Paradise or being saved from Hellfire.

The truly generous person is the one from whom others benefit and he does not seek any recompense for his generosity.

> **Giving Thanks**
>
> The Messenger ﷺ said, *'Whoever is not thankful to people, cannot be thankful to God.'*

The Most Patient (Al-Sabur)

God is Most Patient (al-Sabur) since He does not punish or take revenge immediately from those who deny or disobey Him. He has fixed a time for everything and neither pre-empts nor delays any matter.

In his *Revival of the Religious Sciences*, Imam Ghazali says one who is patient 'does not let hate move him to carry out an action before its time, but rather decides matters according to a definite plan. . .disposing each thing in its proper time, in the way in which it needs to be and according to what it requires.'

For humanity, patience means enduring hardship and difficulty in a calm and composed way and opposing the impulses of passion and anger. To give a few examples, it means waiting calmly for someone, listening receptively to someone's criticism, enduring without complaint illness and injury, bearing with dignity and acceptance of God's decree the news of the death of a loved one.

Divine Attributes

Divine Attributes

KEY POINTS

- God is unique and incomparable, yet the Prophet told us that salvation lies in acquiring the Divine Names – by knowing, loving and emulating them.

- His Names are those of Beauty and Perfection (*asma' al-jamal*) and of Majesty (*asma' al-jalal*).

- For example, by meditating on His Names – the Most Merciful, the Forgiving, the Most Just, the Gentle, the Most Thankful, the Most Generous and the Most Patient – we can seek to bring our character into accordance with the Divine pattern by developing mercy, forgiveness, justice, gentleness, thankfulness, generosity and patience.

Chapter **Four**

Moral Vices

Chapter Four discuss moral vices. These are the habits and characteristics that divide humanity, and create hatred and animosity.

The following table shows the four principle moral vices, their meanings, characteristics and opposites:

The Evil of Arrogance

As mentioned before, Imam Birgivi defines arrogance as the state in which we are convinced that we have the right to be above others. It is an unjustified self-regard in which one compares himself to others and feels superior. Arrogance is unlawful in Islam and is considered to be a disgraceful attitude and sinful behaviour.

Humility is the opposite of arrogance and hence the person can see his own weaknesses and does not talk up his strengths to seek attention.

Only God is Proud as one of His attributes is al-Mutakabbir. No one else has the right to be proud. The arrogant person is likened to the Devil who was proud and refused to prostate before Adam ﷺ. The Devil

Moral Vices

Moral Vice	Meaning	Outcomes/Behaviour	Opposite/s
Arrogance	The conviction that one has the right to be put above others.	Pride, puffed-out chest, disdain, snobbery, nose in the air, superiority complex, vanity, self-importance, self-conceit, narcissism, self-centredness, ostentation, displays of grandeur, exhibitionism, pomposity, boastfulness, bragging, self-glorification, bravado, insolence, haughtiness, contempt, sneering, disrespect	Nobility, Humility, Dignity
Anger	A burst of uncontrolled passion aimed at someone who has hurt you or is threatening to hurt you.	Derision, enmity, hostility, contrariness, quarrelsomeness, unfriendliness, hatred, bitterness, alienation, belligerence	Patience
Envy	The wish to see a person deprived of blessings.	Resentment, discontentedness, possessiveness, hatred, narrow-mindedness, competitiveness, distrustfulness	Compassion, Justice
Greed	The excessive desire for wealth and material things.	Desire, dissatisfaction, yearning, ambition, avarice, gluttony, possessiveness, selfishness	Generosity, Patience

thought he was better than Adam ﷺ since he was made of fire and Adam ﷺ from clay. God cursed him and removed him from his lofty post as a teacher of the angels.

On another occasion he ☀ said, 'The arrogant ones will be locked in coffins of fire and kept there forever.' (Bayhaqi)

What causes arrogance?

Imam Birgivi says that there are seven causes of arrogance: education, piety, lineage, beauty, strength, wealth, achievement (and popularity).

All these seven qualities are in themselves positive and good. However, it is their misuse that leads to arrogance.

If one is proud of his educational credentials and thinks he is better than others then he is a loser. The Messenger ☀ described such people as those 'whose teaching did not do anyone any good'. (Tirmidhi)

The true people of knowledge are those who do not look down upon the ignorant or the sinful. In fact they feel obliged to help by guiding and teaching them. Academic achievement, good exam results, and attending good schools or universities can make some people proud and that feeling of arrogance has

> The Messenger ☀ condemned arrogance and said, 'Whoever has an atom weight of pride in his heart, he will not enter Paradise.' One of the disciples then asked, 'What do you say about someone who dresses in fine clothes?' He ☀ answered, 'God is beautiful and loves beauty. Arrogance is to deny reality and to consider others beneath oneself.'
>
> (Muslim)

to be avoided, but not the pursuit of education itself which is laudable.

The Signs of Arrogance

The following gestures, activities and desires are clear signs of arrogance:

1. The wish to be recognised as someone important whom people should stand up for or salute.
2. Not wishing to sit next to someone you consider to be beneath you.
3. Failing to do menial tasks like cleaning up, washing clothes, etc.
4. Feeling embarrassed when carrying out a household errand in public or shopping at cheap marketplaces.
5. Not accepting the invitation of the poor.

Tackling Arrogance

The tried and tested cure for this moral sickness lies in becoming humble. This means knowing oneself as accurately as possible: Who am I? Where do I come from? Where am I going? What's the purpose of life?

One must know facts about oneself rather than believe in fantasies of the ego. The problem with the ego is that it's neither rational nor pious. It tends towards exaggeration and seeks delude you and others. It thinks highly of itself and sets itself above others. If one is humble, one believes oneself to be less than the eye of the ego makes one out to be.

The Messenger ﷺ said, 'When someone is humble to his fellow Muslim, God raises that person's state. On the other hand when someone belittles a fellow Muslim and claims to be better, God lowers that person far below the others.' (Tabarani)

Humility is a great virtue that makes a person listen to others. This willingness to listen to others is a key to mutual understanding, from which arises a peaceful society.

The Vice of Anger

Anger is a burst of uncontrolled passion aimed at someone who has hurt you or is threatening to hurt you. It is a vengeful attack with the aim of destroying the perceived enemy by punishing him severely. Such bursts of anger or fury can be extremely harmful to the angry person as well as to his or her victim. Fury potentially makes a person mindless and violent. However, anger is sometimes necessary to protect the weak and for standing up for justice.

The opposites of anger are patience and gentleness. These qualities enable a person to remain calm and to control himself instead of raving and being aggressive. Anger tends to create violence whilst patience and gentleness tend to lead towards compassion and peace.

> The Messenger ﷺ said, *'Surely God has ordered us to be humble. I tell you that none among you shall belittle any other, nor are you permitted to insult them.'*
>
> (Abu Dawud)

There are many benefits of overcoming anger:

1. God praises people who are able to overcome anger as He says, *Those who overcome anger and forgive people, God loves such righteous people.* (Al 'Imran 3:134)

2. God will not punish anyone who abandons anger. The Messenger ﷺ said, 'God will abandon punishing the one who can overcome his anger.' (Tabarani)

3. The Prophet ﷺ said, 'Whoever has these qualities will receive God's mercy: being thankful to God; forgiving instead of punishing when one is wronged; restraining oneself from expressing one's anger and hurting people.' (Hakim)

Causes of anger

Anger can be caused by a number of triggers, for instance someone's tyrannical behaviour like harming people or treating them unjustly. One should not allow such things and the best way to deal with tyrannical people is to seek the help of others.

Anger can be caused by bad jokes, criticism or opposition to one's opinions. In these situations, one needs to be strong and ignore the jests of the ignorant.

Another cause of anger is excessive worldly desire or ambition. When one's desire or ambition is not fulfilled, then one becomes angry. When one sees the wealthy in their pomp, wearing the latest designer fashions, one wants to be like them. When one can't get what they have, one becomes angry.

Anger can be triggered by badly-behaved children or poorly trained and incompetent officials to give a few examples. It is unreasonable to react angrily in such situations since it is not their fault. Worst still is getting angry at machinery and gadgets when they don't work properly: these things have no consciousness, will or intention.

One of the worst kinds of anger is to be angry with God. This may arise because of a natural disaster or illness, when one considers oneself to have been singled out. It could also arise when someone uses the Qur'an and the Prophetic traditions to argue with and criticise a person. May God protect us from such anger.

How to control anger

1. The first strategy is to seek God's protection from Satan. Sulayman ibn Surayd ﷺ said: 'Once two men cursed one another in the presence of the Messenger ﷺ: their faces were red with anger. The Messenger ﷺ said to them, "I knew a phrase that if you had said it, your anger would have disappeared. It is *ta'widh*: 'I seek God's protection from Satan the rejected.'"' (Bukhari)

2. The second way to overcome anger is to sit down if one is standing up or to lie down if one is sitting up. (Abu Dawud)

3. Performing the ritual ablution (*wudu'*) with cold water will also help to reduce anger. The Messenger ﷺ said, 'Anger comes from Satan and Satan is created from fire. Fire can only be put out by water. So whenever one of you is angry, let him perform the ritual ablution.' (Abu Dawud)

65

4. Another way of controlling one's anger is to realise and understand the merits and excellence of doing so. The Prophet ﷺ has praised those who can control themselves. He ﷺ said, 'Musa ﷺ asked God, "Who do you love the most?" God replied, "The one who forgives yet he knows he has the power to take revenge." ' (Tabrizi) On another occasion, he ﷺ described the strong person as 'one who can control his anger'. (Bukhari)

The Evil of Envy

Envy is the wish to see a person one dislikes deprived of a blessing, although the blessing that other person has does not in any way affect him. Envy is forbidden in Islam. However, unintentional envy is considered to be excusable.

The Messenger ﷺ warned against envy: 'Beware of envy. It burns to ashes one's good deeds.' (Abu Dawud)

The Glorious Qur'an advises people to seek Divine protection from *the evil of the envier*. (al-Falaq 113:5)

Dangers of Envy

Why does the Messenger ﷺ say that 'envy destroys all the rewards of good deeds'? The answer lies in the dangerous nature of this moral vice. It leads to the following:

1. Disobedience to God since the envier is gossiping, cursing and unnecessarily frightening his victim. It is a kind of tyranny.

2. The envier's evil effects can sometimes be disastrous for the envied. The Qur'an teaches us to seek God's refuge from the envier just as we seek His refuge from Devil's temptations. The Messenger ﷺ said, 'When you receive in abundance from your Lord that which you needed, keep it secret. For anyone who is thus blessed will suffer the envy of others.' (Tabarani)

3. Envy causes grief and severe anxiety to the envier. He suffers badly at his own hands.

Causes of Envy

Vengeance is a destructive force of hatred that destroys people. It urges us not only to feel justified but even obliged to destroy our enemy. Islam condemns such vengeance and instead teaches tolerance and for-giveness.

Egotism is to believe in one's personal superiority and that, as a result, one is entitled to preferential treatment. Such a person cannot bear the thought of seeing anyone else attaining more wealth, honour, knowledge or status than him or her. The solution to this is that he should not compare himself to those who are superior to him, thinking himself unfortunate, but instead he should look at those who are less fortunate than him so that he may be thankful for the blessings that he has.

Arrogance can also lead to envy. An arrogant person's pride is not justified by his qualities or abilities. So when he sees someone truly possessing those qualities, he fears that his rival may get the upper hand, so he wishes that his competitor loses them. This competition is common amongst members of any organisation, whether private or public, secular or religious.

Being negative about everything around oneself is also another cause of envy. These sorts of enviers are neither arrogant nor jealous: they just suffer when they hear someone else being praised or on hearing good news. It is as though the good someone else has received was taken away from these enviers personally. This sickness is the worst kind of envy.

The Evil of Greed

Greed is the excessive desire for wealth and worldly things. The Messenger ﷺ said, 'The worst traits found in people are greed and cowardice.' (Abu Dawud)

Why are people greedy? It basically stems from a lack of faith in God as our Sustainer. The greedy person thinks his future sustenance is in his own hands. Therefore, he must gather as much it as he can. Another reason for excessive attachment to the world is family and children. Again his greed leads him to forget that it is his Generous Lord Who ultimately provides for his children. While parents always have a duty of care towards their children, it is God who provides for them.

Another reason for greed is the desire to gather wealth for its own sake and to keep it locked away. That wealth is not just locked away but its love fills the heart with so much greed that there is no room left to love anything else. The following Qur'anic passage describes the reality of the world:

Always remember that the life of this world is play and amusement, pomp and mutual boasting about your children and wealth. It is like the rain which causes the vegetation to grow, pleasing the farmer, then it withers away, turning yellow. And in the Hereafter is a severe punishment. (al-Hadid 57:20)

Greed affects human behaviour drastically and it makes a person miserly or a spendthrift. God says:

And let not those who are miserly in spending that which God has granted them think that it is good for them. Nay it is evil for them. They shall have a collar of their miserliness on their necks on the Day of Resurrection. God's is the heritage of the heavens and the earth. (Al 'Imran 3:180)

God says, *O believers, let not your wealth and children divert you from the remembrance of God, whoever does so will surely be a loser.* (al-Munafiqun 63:9)

Imam Mawlud gives advice on how to cure greed:

'Reflect long and hard on the fact that just as people climb the heights of affluence and start to achieve what they have worn out themselves for, then death assails them. Our wealth stays behind for others to wrangle over and spend.' He also reminds us that misers are the most despised, and people hate them. This should be enough to turn one away from this evil. (H. Yusuf, *Purification of the Heart*)

Moral Vices

KEY POINTS

- The four principal vices are arrogance, anger, envy and greed.

- Arrogance is the belief that one has the right to be put over others. Its opposite and cure is humility.

- Anger is a burst of uncontrolled passion directed at someone who has hurt you or threatens to do so. It is the anger that arouses the ego which is blameworthy and not the anger aroused by injustice which is praiseworthy. Its opposite and cure is patience and gentleness that leads to compassion and peace.

- Envy is the intentional wish to deprive another of a blessing. Its cures and opposites are compassion for others and a sense of justice.

- Greed is the excessive desire for wealth and material things. Its opposites and cures are generosity with one's possessions and having patient faith in God as our Sustainer.

Chapter **Five**

Seven Steps to Moral Intelligence

So far we have covered morality, moral virtues and vices, the Divine moral attributes and how the Messenger ﷺ loved and lived by them. But how do we acquire and develop these wonderful moral virtues? In this, the central chapter of the book, we look at the seven steps towards moral intelligence.

Step One: Setting the Goal

In order to succeed in attaining moral intelligence, a clear goal must be set. That goal is to develop good character, and Ghazali begins by describing the excellence and merits of good character:

Certainly your character [i.e. the Prophet's] *is most sublime.* (al-Qalam 68:4)

Whoever has purified his heart has succeeded and whoever has corrupted it is a loser. (al-Shams 91:9-10)

Then he quotes thirty-five *Ahadith*, which describe and praise the excellence of developing good character. Some of these *Ahadith* are mentioned below:

'A'ishah ﷺ was asked about the Prophet's ﷺ character. She said, 'His character was the Qur'an.' (Muslim)

A man once asked: 'What is religion?' He ﷺ replied 'Good character.' He then came from the right and asked the same question. The Messenger ﷺ gave exactly the same reply. He again came from the left and asked the same question and the Messenger ﷺ gave the same response. He came from behind and got the same response. Finally the Messenger ﷺ said, 'Have you not grasped it? It is that you do not become angry.' (Mundhiri)

Once the Messenger ﷺ was asked: 'What is an ill omen (*shu'm*)?' He ﷺ replied, 'Bad character.' (Abu Dawud, Ibn Hanbal)

He ﷺ was asked, 'Which was the best of deeds?' and he ﷺ replied, 'To have good character.' (Zabidi)

The Prophet ﷺ was once told about a certain woman who fasted all day and prayed all night but had bad character so that she injured her neighbours with her words. 'There is no good in her', he ﷺ said, 'she is of Hell's people.' (Ibn Hanbal)

He ﷺ said, 'You will not be able to give gifts to all the people with your wealth, however you can treat them with a cheerful smile and good character.' (Abu Ya'la)

A prayer of the Prophet ﷺ was, 'O Lord, you have made my appearance beautiful, therefore make good my character.' (Ibn Hanbal)

Anas ﷺ said: 'One day we were with the Messenger ﷺ and he said, "Good character melts away sin just as the sun melts ice."' (Tabarani)

Imam Ghazali then cites several reports concerning the early Muslims.

Wahb ibn Munabbih said, 'The man of bad character is like a broken pot that can neither be patched up nor returned to clay.' And it has been said, 'Every building has a foundation and the foundation of Islam is good character.'

Step One is about realising the value of good character and being motivated to develop it and making this the goal. Ghazali provides ample proof of the worth and value of making this a lifetime goal.

Step Two: Understanding Good and Bad Character

Once you have set your sights on developing good character then you need to make preparations for it. This begins by understanding the nature of good character and being convinced that it can be changed. These are Steps Two and Three which help one to really get to know his or her goal.

Ghazali says that while many people have discussed the true nature of good character, they have only treated its fruits and not its reality, and they have not successfully defined it. He gives examples of how people have defined the concept of good character:

Hasan al-Basri, the great scholar and Sufi, said, 'Good character is a cheerful face, magnanimity, and doing no harm.'

Al-Wasti said, 'It is to please people secretly and in public.'

Ghazali says, 'Creation (*khalq*) and character (*khuluq*) are two terms; creation refers to the external form and character to the internal form.' He then gives a definition, 'A trait of character, then, is a firmly-established condition of the heart from which actions proceed easily without any need for thinking.' According to this definition, if one does a beautiful deed, then it is termed good character, and, on the other hand, if one performs an ugly act, then it is bad character.

An example of this is a man who gives charity now and then but has doubt as to whether he should give it or not! Even if he gives he can't be described as generous, as true generosity should proceed from a person easily without hesitation or doubt.

According to Ghazali, good character has four parts:

1. Doing a beautiful act
2. Having the ability to act
3. Being aware of the act
4. The inclination of the heart towards either the beautiful or the ugly which makes the act easy to carry out.

Ghazali makes an important distinction when he says, 'Therefore character is not the same as action.'

For example, there are many people of generous character who do not make donations because they don't have any money. Just as there are many miserly and greedy people who will give charity but for some other motive like vanity. So Ghazali argues that, 'Character, therefore, is a term for the condition and inner aspect of the heart.'

The four cardinal traits of good character are:

1. Wisdom
2. Courage

3. Temperance
4. Justice

All others are branches of these four.

Ghazali distinguishes between the outward signs of good character and its true nature which he regards as the state of heart being inclined towards doing good.

Step Three: You Really Can Change Yourself!

A person is a complex handiwork of *both* nature and nurture, *both* chromosomes and culture. In his *Revival of the Religious Sciences*, Ghazali accepts this interplay of biology and upbringing but emphasises the power of human free will: 'A lazy and careless person will be reluctant to reform his character claiming that character cannot be altered, just like a person cannot alter his appearance (*khalq*) he is unable to alter his character (*khuluq*).'

Secondly he will assert that good character requires suppressing one's desire and anger and that he has tested this by doing so, but as it didn't work, it was a waste of time. Ghazali rejects this claim and says, 'If change in traits of character was not possible then why would God have sent Messengers to teach, preach, give sermons and discipline people?' The Messenger ﷺ said, 'Improve your character.' (Zabidi) This clearly implies that human characteristics can be changed for the better.

Even the character of animals can be changed: take the falcon or the dog that can be trained for hunting or a wild stallion that can be trained to become a good riding horse.

He then says that all created things can be divided into two groups. Firstly, things that cannot be changed: the sky, the stars and even human appearance and, secondly, things that are susceptible to change, that are incomplete and can be perfected. A seed is an example: it can become a tree if it is provided with the right conditions for growth. Similarly, we can influence our own anger and desire should we so wish by means of self-discipline and struggle. However the speed and degree to which we can alter character varies for two reasons. Firstly, the longer the instinct (*gharizah*) has been present and left untouched the more difficult it becomes to change it. Secondly, there is complacency, meaning that one is satisfied with things remaining the same. Ghazali divides complacent people into four groups:

1. Those innocently ignorant and unaware of right and wrong – and living in their natural state (*fitrah*). They are open to changing rapidly.
2. Those who are ignorant and misguided recognise right and wrong but act wrongly because evil appeals to them. They are influenced by their desires and are aware of their wrongdoings. They too can reform themselves but their task is more difficult that the first group.
3. Those who are ignorant, misguided and corrupt, and who consider ugly traits to be preferable since they have been brought up with no sense of right and wrong. It is almost impossible to reform such people.
4. Those who are ignorant, misguided, corrupt and evil, who have been brought up to believe in and

to work for corruption. These are the most difficult to reform.

Ghazali also challenges the commonly-held notion that anger, desire, worldliness and other traits of this kind cannot be removed from the heart.

This is an error, he says, as spiritual struggle is not about uprooting and obliterating these traits – such a view is absurd because desire has been created for a purpose and is an indispensable part of human nature. For example, if one did not feel hungry, then one would die; if there were no sexual desire, then the human species would become extinct; if there were no anger, then one would not be able to guard and defend oneself. So the reform of character is not about removing these traits, rather it's about restoring them to their right balance and proportion.

Ghazali gives examples to prove this point:

Anger has two extremes of recklessness and cowardice, and reforming anger means that the intellect is able to control it.

Regarding greed and extravagance the Qur'an says, *and those who, when they spend, are neither extravagant nor miserly and there is ever a middle point between the two* (al-Furqan 25:6-7) and *eat and drink but be not extravagant for God loves not the extravagant* (al-A'raf 7:31). The Messenger ﷺ said, 'The best of affairs is the middle course.' (Maydani)

Ghazali comes back to the principle that character can indeed be changed – the idea is not to rid the heart of desire, anger and worldliness but to bring it to the middle course, so that it is equidistant from the two extremes. Generosity is the midpoint between greed and extravagance. Courage is the midpoint between cowardice and recklessness.

Temperance, meaning moderation and self-restraint, is the midpoint between acquisitiveness and indifference. It is rather the extremes that are reprehensible.

Step Three is about conviction, or being convinced beyond doubt that human character can be changed – it does not need to be removed altogether but reformed.

Step Four: Looking for Faults in Yourself

By now the traveller is motivated and understands the nature of good character and believes that human character can be changed. Step Four is about getting started on this journey.

Ghazali uses another example. Every body-part has been created for a specific function, however when it falls ill it is unable to carry out that function. The eye sees and the hand grasps. The function of the heart is the acquisition of knowledge, wisdom, experiential knowledge and love of God, and of His worship and taking delight in remembering Him and preferring all these things to every other desire.

The sign of the experiential knowledge of God is love of Him and this love is demonstrated by preferring Him more than worldly things.

So what is the sickness of the heart? It is to prefer things over the love of God. Therefore the symptom of this sickness is simply to prefer all these worldly things over the love of God (may He be Exalted).

Ghazali then comes back to the definition of good character as the middle course since it is at this point that the heart is furthest from the two extremes. For example, if a person is greedy, then he must give in charity so that he establishes a balance between greed and extravagance.

Thus the traveller stays on the middle course, far from the two extremes, which requires enormous effort. This he calls the Straight Path (*sirat al-mustaqim*). Due to the difficulty of remaining on the Straight Path, we are required to pray constantly, *guide us on the Straight Path*, at least seventeen times a day during our daily prayers.

Ghazali observes that through Divine Grace a person can see his own faults; however, the vast majority of people remain blind to their own faults. Therefore he suggests four methods of discovering the faults of the soul:

1. **Going to an experienced spiritual director (*shaykh al-tasawwuf*) who has insight into these faults and weaknesses.** One must follow his guidance and instructions in treating these inner faults. However, Ghazali lamented that there were few such people in his age, and, as he was speaking of the eleventh century, what of our own twenty-first century?)

2. **Seeking advice from a critical friend.** This he recommends as a powerful means of discovering one's inner faults. He gives the example of 'Umar ﷺ who would ask Salman ﷺ to pick out his faults and inform him of them. However, this is not always possible because too many friends are flatterers

and therefore conceal your faults from you. In Ghazali's view it is instead better to seek the advice of a friend who is jealous of you for he or she will more readily reveal your faults to you. A well-known Sufi, Dawud al-Ta'i, used to say, 'What can I do with people who hide my faults from me?' Sadly, the most hateful of all people are those who counsel us and draw our attention to our defects.

3. **Learn the faults of one's soul by listening to the statements of one's enemies since a hostile eye picks out defects.** Although the common tendency will be to disbelieve and dismiss the observation of the foe, the insightful person will derive benefit from it.

4. **Mixing with all sorts of people.** Ghazali suggests when you see faults in other people you should ascribe them to yourself as well because 'the believers are mirrors to one another'. You may ascribe the faults of others to yourself on the basis that people's temperaments are similar with regard to the following of their desires. So people tend to develop similar faults, even if they will differ in the degree to which they are developed. This can therefore be an effective means of cleansing oneself of evil traits.

So only by finding out one's weaknesses or faults can one take the corrective steps, so this self-assessment is vitally important.

Step Five: Renouncing Your Desires

For Ghazali, the first principle in curing the sicknesses of the heart lies in renouncing your desires. He cites verses of the Glorious Qur'an, traditions of the Prophet and the anecdotes of religious scholars to prove his point.

The Qur'an says:

He who feared the meeting with his Lord and restrained himself from base desires, Paradise will be his home. (al-Nazi'at 79:40-41)

The self (*nafs*) is the active and creative force within the individual that seeks expression, development and growth.

The Messenger ﷺ said, 'The believer is beset with five afflictions: a believer who envies him; a hypocrite who hates him; an unbeliever who makes war on him; a devil who misguides him; and the self which struggles against him.' (Abu Bakr ibn Lal)

When some disciples were returning to Madinah from a jihad, the Messenger ﷺ welcomed them and said, 'You have come from the lesser to the greater jihad.' They replied, 'O Messenger of God, what is the greater jihad?' 'The jihad against the self', he ﷺ replied. (al-Bukhari, *al-Adab al-Mufrad*)

The Messenger ﷺ said, 'The real warrior (*mujahid*) is the one who fights with himself for the sake of God.' (Ibn Hanbal)

Yahya ibn Mu'adh al-Razi, the famous scholar of Hadith, said, 'Fight your self with swords of self-discipline, and these are four: eating little, sleeping briefly, speaking only when necessary, and tolerating all the wrongs done to you by men.' He also said, 'Man has three enemies: the world, the Devil and the self. Be on your guard against the world through renunciation, against the Devil by disobeying him and against the ego by abandoning desire.'

The Sufi Malik ibn Dinar used to roam the market place and whenever he saw something that he desired, he would say to himself, 'Be patient, for I swear by God that I only deny you because of the esteem in which I hold you.'

Ghazali is so certain of his view that the only remedy of sicknesses of the heart is giving up desire that he is prepared to say that 'to believe in this is therefore an obligation'. He then asks why this is so and therefore defines the essence and the secret of self-discipline as being, 'that the soul should not take pleasure in anything that will not be present in the grave, in matters of food, marriage, clothing and accommodation and every other thing that one needs, and one should restrict oneself to what is necessary and indispensable.'

Ghazali advises that one should pre-occupy himself with the love of God and anything that strengthens that good attachment with the Lord. He then classifies people into four groups:

1. Those whose hearts are engrossed in God's remembrance so that they only fulfil the bare minimum of worldly needs. These are the Truthful (*al-siddiqun*).
2. Those whose hearts are engrossed in the world and they remember God only mechanically, doing so with the tongue rather than with the heart.
3. Those whose hearts are occupied by both God and the world, however, their hearts are still more inclined towards God. Perhaps they will spend brief periods in Hell before being admitted to Heaven.

4. Those whose hearts are engrossed with both God and the world but attachment to the world predominates. They will remain in Hellfire for a much longer period.

Ghazali provides arguments for renouncing the delights of the world. He says since these are only temporary and that one has to leave them at the time of death one may either suffer at their departure or instead remain pre-occupied with God and good works that will persist and accompany one in the grave. But the sad reality is that people spend their lives denying their morality and the hollow reality behind their worldly works and ambitions. Ghazali suggests that an intelligent person can see that this is a fleeting world, a very short probationary period compared with the eternity of the Hereafter.

Although the method of discipline and struggle varies from person to person the basic principle remains the same. It is namely that 'all should renounce those things of the world which are found to be pleasurable.' As a test he points out that if one rejoices in the pleasure of wealth, fame, intelligence, appearance, and so on then one should renounce these and remain in seclusion until such time that the heart gets used to the remembrance of God. One should persevere with this and continue with this greater Jihad, the Jihad against one's self, until death.

Step Five is the critical stage in moral development according to Ghazali. This step prepares the traveller to begin sculpting one's character, defining it with good attributes.

Step Six: Developing Good Character

After explaining the nature of good character and the fact that it can be changed if one so wishes, Ghazali proceeds to outline three means by which good character may be acquired.

1. Practice makes perfect

Constant and regular practice over time helps one to become accustomed and familiar with good character. There are many examples one might give. A medical student who wants to become a qualified doctor will have to study and train long and hard before he or she is granted permission to practice medicine. A gambler, despite loosing often, becoming poorer and piling up debts, will enjoy his pastime as he is so attracted to it. A rock climber will face all sorts of bad weather and testing physical challenges so much does he wish to excel at the sport that he loves. So familiarity and acquaintance with a particular skill, hobby or interest makes it all the more easy and enjoyable. So Ghazali argues that good character can also be acquired by constant practice and familiarity. Likewise to become generous, one must do it again and again until it becomes a habit. One must accustom oneself to the practice of beautiful character.

2. Keeping the company of righteous people

The Messenger ﷺ said, 'A person follows the religion of his friend so beware who your friends are.' (al-Tabrizi)

3. The need for a spiritual director (*shaykh al-tasawwuf*)

Ghazali argues that a person without a shaykh will probably be misguided by the Devil. The person who doesn't have a shaykh is like a traveller crossing a desert without a guide, he is most likely to get lost. He compares a person without a shaykh to a wild tree that is neither pruned nor cross-fertilised which, as a consequence, does not bear fruit, and to a blind man walking along the bank of a river without a guide – he could fall into the river and drown.

The shaykh provides a refuge for the seeker and gives him instructions that act like a shield protecting him from loss. This shield is built from four things:

1. Solitude
2. Silence
3. Hunger
4. Sleeplessness

The seeker's purpose is to mend his heart so as to draw near to his Lord. How do these four practices cure the sickness of the heart and develop good character?

Ghazali says:

'Hunger reduces the quantity of blood, softens the heart and makes it difficult for the Devil to flow in the veins. Sleeplessness also clears, purifies and illuminates the heart. Sleeplessness is also the consequence of hunger. One tip for reducing sleep is not to drink too much water. As for silence this is facilitated by being isolated (being in solitude) thus avoiding unnecessary distraction.'

The traveller is now adequately equipped to embark on the journey to God, armed with the above shield, guided by the shaykh and with a genuine aspiration that he or she can march forward on the Straight Path.

By now the seeker (*murid*) is free from the burden of the barriers of wealth, status, worldliness and sin.

The inner Jihad and the disciplining of the self can now proceed as the seeker opposes his desire, rejects his whims and disobeys his ego. He or she fulfils the obligatory duties and eagerly carries out the voluntary ones. The shaykh will also give her or him certain invocations to praise and remember God called *awrad* to repeat throughout the day and night.

The love of God grows, blossoms and the seeker is in passionate love with her or his Lord. As the seeker progresses spiritually, the obstacle of distraction (*khawatir*) rears its ugly head. These are irrelevant thoughts that come at random to the mind and can destroy concentration.

Ghazali then outlines how a shaykh will continue to monitor, assess and instruct the seeker, and the methodology used by the shaykh may in fact closely mirror what was Ghazali's own practice for training his disciples.

Regular remembrance of God (*dhikr*) and persistence in reforming oneself whilst keeping the company of righteous people attracts the Divine Grace and leads to the acquisition of noble character.

Ghazali employs the metaphor of bodily health and sickness for the health and sickness of the self. Just like a good physician will treat bodily illnesses with an appropriate amount of medicine, so the spiritual director (*shaykh al-tasawwuf*), who is the physician of the heart, must give specific guidance and individualised instruction.

Ghazali gives examples of how various bad characteristics will be treated by the shaykh. If the seeker is ignorant, then the shaykh will teach him the basics of cleanliness and the performance of devotions. If the seeker earns a living, then the shaykh will tell him to forsake any work which involves unlawful means like selling alcohol. If the seeker is very wealthy, then the shaykh will encourage him to give in charity. If the seeker is full of pride and vanity, he will be told to humiliate himself in public in some way so as to destroy his pride, for instance, to beg in the street. Normally begging is discouraged but in this instance it is done to get rid of the greater sin of pride. If the seeker is vain and conscious of his looks, then the shaykh will make him clean latrines or work in the kitchen to break his vanity. If the seeker loves to overeat, then the shaykh will direct him to fast more and also moderate his eating. If the seeker has a high sex drive, then the shaykh instructs him to fast more regularly and avoid eating rich foods like meat. If the seeker is cowardly, then the shaykh will strengthen his courage by directing him to physical challenges like setting sail in rough seas during the winter. If the seeker is lazy in worship, then the shaykh will direct him to do more voluntary worship like performing the night prayers (*tahajjud*).

In brief, the general technique of the shaykh consists in doing the opposite of everything that the self inclines to and craves. For God says, *And whoever fears the standing before his Lord and forbids his soul its whim, for him Heaven shall be the place of resort.* (al-Nazi'at 79:41-42)

The basic principle in spiritual struggle is to carry out what one wants to achieve, so if one is determined to renounce a desire then God will make it easier for him to let go of it.

Step Six involves the ongoing practising of good habits and living with people of God and waiting for Divine grace in order that good character is granted.

Step Seven: Reviewing Your Progress

'Good character is equivalent to faith,' says Ghazali, and 'bad character to hypocrisy.' So it's important to identify these signs so that these can be nurtured. There are several Qur'anic passages which enumerate these noble traits, for example:

The believers have triumphed: who are humble in their prayers, who avoid vain activities, who pay zakah, who guard their chastity, and who observe their pledge and covenant. (al-Mu'minun 23:1–3)

Those who repent, worship, praise, fast, bow, prostrate, enjoin good, forbid evil and keep limits ordained by God and give glad tidings to the believers. (al-Ahzab 33:112)

Those whose hearts tremble with fear when God is mentioned, and who when signs of God are recited to them grow in faith and who trust in their Lord; those who establish the prayer and spend of that which we have bestowed upon them. Such are true believers. (al-Anfal 8:1-2)

The slaves of the Merciful are those who walk gently on the earth and who when the foolish address them answer peace. (al-Furqan 25:63)

One should measure his character against these nineteen characteristics of true believers: the more one has of these traits, the better. These are what the Messenger, ﷺ refers to as the moral virtues (*mahasin al-akhlaq*).

The Messenger ﷺ was asked about the distinguishing marks of the believer and the hypocrite. He ﷺ replied, 'The believer's concern is for prayer, fasting and worship, while the hypocrite, like an animal, is concerned with food and drink.' (Zabidi)

Islam firmly embeds the traits of good character in the doctrine of the Oneness of God (*tawhid*) and the life hereafter, and therefore these traits are not mere humanistic values but Divine. The early Muslims attempted to live by these lofty ideals and they embellished themselves with these traits.

The Sufi Hatim al-Asamm said: 'The believer is occupied with devotion while the hypocrite is occupied with greed and

---

The Signs of Good Character

The believer loves for his brother what he loves for himself.

(Bukhari)

Whosoever believes in God and the Last Day should honour his guest.

(Bukhari and Muslim)

Whosoever believes in God and the Last Day should honour his neighbour.

(Bukhari)

Whosoever believes in God and the Last Day should say something good or stay silent.

(Bukhari)

The man who is made joyful by his good deeds and sad by his evil works is a believer.

(Ibn Hanbal)

his hopes. The believer has despaired of everyone but God, whilst the hypocrite has set his hopes in everyone except Him. The believer sets his religion before money while the hypocrite sets money before his religion. The believer does good and weeps while the hypocrite does evil and laughs. The believer loves solitude and isolation while the hypocrite loves company and assemblies.'

Ghazali says that one test of good character is nature of one's response to suffering and the offence given by others. He then provides examples of how people of good character respond to bad treatment. Once the Messenger ﷺ was walking with Anas ؓ when a nomad came up to him and pulled his Najrani cloak so violently that it left red marks on his neck. The nomad then demanded, 'O Muhammad! Give me some of God's money which you have.' The Messenger ﷺ turned to him smiling and ordered that he be given some money.

Ghazali tells a story of Abu 'Uthman who was one day riding in the street when a pot of ash was thrown over him. He got down, prostrated and thanked God. People asked, 'Are you not going to rebuke him?' He simply said, 'A man who deserves Hellfire but only receives ashes cannot be angry.'

A woman once said to Malik ibn Dinar, 'You hypocrite!' And he said, 'Woman! You have found my name which everyone else in Basra has mislaid.'

These are the seven steps of moral development. By knowing them, and applying them you can achieve good character, *insha'Allah*.

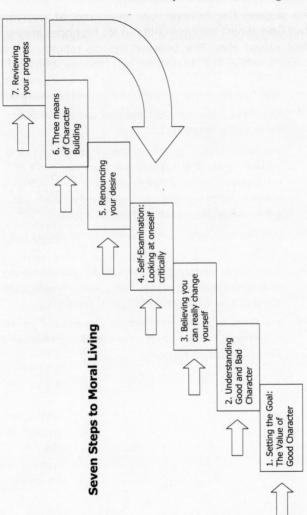

Seven Steps to Moral Living

1. Setting the Goal: The Value of Good Character

2. Understanding Good and Bad Character

3. Believing you can really change yourself

4. Self-Examination: Looking at oneself critically

5. Renouncing your desire

6. Three means of Character Building

7. Reviewing your progress

KEY POINTS

- Step One is setting a clear goal of moral development for oneself.

- Step Two is understanding what is good and bad character.

- Step Three is believing that character can be changed for the better by reforming it.

- Step Four is examining one's own character by understanding one's faults. One may seek help to do this from a spiritual director (*shaykh al-tasawwuf*), seeking advice from a critical friend or even from an enemy, and comparing oneself in relation to all kinds of different people.

- Step Five is to better one's character by controlling one's desires.

- Step Six is to develop good character by practising doing what is right, keeping good company and by following the advice of a spiritual director (*shaykh al-tasawwuf*).

- Step Seven is continuing to monitor and measure oneself by reference to the highest standards of good character and to the traits of hypocrisy.

Chapter **Six**

Ghazali's Moral Intelligence

His name was Abu Hamid ibn Muhammad ibn Muhammad al-Tusi al-Shafi'i al-Ghazali and he was honoured with the title of the 'Proof of Islam' (*Hujjat al-Islam*).

He was born in 1058 CE (450 AH) in the town of Tabran in the district of Tus situated within the province of Khorasan (an historic region that covered parts of modern-day Afghanistan, Iran, Tajikistan, Turkmenistan and Uzbekistan). His father was a cotton merchant and therefore he is referred to as Ghazali. His early education was from local teachers in his home town. He then moved to Jurjan and studied under Imam Abu Nasr Isma'ili.

The young Ghazali was a brilliant student with an incisive wit and sharp intellect. In those days, there were many schools and colleges in every major town and city; however, Nishapur and Baghdad were among the most famous. As Nishapur was closer to home, Imam Ghazali decided to go there. Here al-Juwayni, known as Imam al-Haramayn, taught students the Islamic sciences.

Imam Ghazali soon earned a special place amongst the students of Imam al-Haramayn, and was appointed as an assistant teacher. Ghazali began to write and his teacher encouraged him in this endeavour. Soon his fame began to spread. It was around this time that Imam Ghazali was initiated into the spiritual order of Shaykh Farmadi.

When Imam al-Juwayni died in 1086 CE (475 AH), Imam Ghazali decided to leave Nishapur and head for Baghdad. This was the other great centre of learning, then under the patronage of Nizam al-Mulk, who had built the great Nizamiyyah University in the city.

Imam Ghazali in Baghdad

Imam Ghazali was appointed as a teacher at this prestigious institution. Nizam al-Mulk was an erudite scholar himself and loved the company of scholars and his court was like a debating society. This provided young scholars an opportunity not only to show off their debating skills and depth of scholarship but to impress the royals.

Imam Ghazali came to love the pomp and ceremony of these occasions and it wasn't long before his genius became apparent: his debates, lectures and counselling were overwhelmingly impressive.

His brilliance in all branches of learning became well-established and Nizam al-Mulk recognised this when, in 1092 CE, Imam Ghazali was appointed the head of Nizamiyyah at the young age of 34. This was one of the highest ranking civil positions at the most prestigious place of learning in the capital of Nizam al-Mulk's empire. Imam Ghazali had come to have a lot of influence on the royal family: they listened to him and heeded his advice. His fame, wealth, reputation and influence were at their zenith. He lived a life of luxury and was showered with every conceivable worldly honour and privilege.

Imam Ghazali had wide-ranging interests, but philosophy and spirituality were his favourite subjects. As his interest in spirituality deepened, he became critical of all the pomp, wealth and status and a conflict began to brew inside him. He felt like leaving Baghdad and retiring into obscurity. 'For six months,' Imam Ghazali writes of this tense period in his autobiography, 'I was in [such] a state of tremendous anxiety [that I reached the stage that] I could neither speak, nor eat, nor teach. Eventually I became ill, and the physicians declared me untreatable.' He wrote,

'I came to the conclusion that the blessings of the Hereafter cannot be attained without piety (*taqwa*) and giving up carnal desires. And this can only happen once the love of the world disappears, until one renounces the world and yearns for the Hereafter. Man must energetically and completely turn to his Lord. And this cannot happen without giving up pomp and wealth. When I examined myself, I found myself deeply attached to the world. When I studied the motives behind my lecturing, I found it was merely for grandeur and status. I was now convinced that I stood at the brink of disaster. I reflected on this state for a long time. One day I would decide to leave Baghdad and free myself of these shackles, but the next day I would change my mind. I would take one step forward and another backward. In the morning, I would yearn for the Hereafter but, by the evening, those thoughts would be overwhelmed by worldly desires. The chains of carnal desires would pull upon me and the voice of faith would say, "Go! Go! Only a few hours of life remain yet the journey is long, your works are merely for showing off and delusion. If you do not prepare for the Hereafter now when will you do so?" Finally, I decided to leave Baghdad. The scholars and the government officials pleaded with me to take back my decision saying, "This will be bad luck for the Muslims – how can your departure be justifiable in Islam?" Whilst everyone was saying this, I knew the truth and therefore left for Syria.' (*al-Munqidh min al-Dalal – Deliverance from Error*)

This crisis occurred in 1096 CE (488 AH).

The Epic Journey of Self-Discovery

Ghazali travelled to Damascus to live in solitude and spent his time in devotion and self-purification. He would climb the western minaret of the Grand Umayyad Mosque and remain there all day, submerged in Divine remembrance and meditation. He would also teach in the western wing of the Grand Mosque. After two years of devotion and spiritual exercises, he moved to Jerusalem and stayed at the Dome of the Rock.

From there he went to the town of Khalif in the West Bank. At the tomb of Prophet Ibrahim ﷺ, he made three pledges:

1. Never to visit a royal court
2. Never to accept royal gifts
3. Never to debate with anyone

From there he decided to perform the Hajj. For ten long years, he remained on his journey of self-discovery and search for truth, wondering through deserts, jungles, cities and mountains, and often stayed near the tombs of the saints. During this time, Imam Ghazali wrote books and taught in various seminaries and guided many students. After this decade of wayfaring and acquiring a deeper understanding of Islam, he once again returned to Baghdad. He was received with joy and offered the mantle of Rector of the Nizamiyyah once more. It is thought that it was here that he wrote his greatest work, *The Revival of the Religious Sciences*, which is one of the classics of Islamic scholarship. Imam Ghazali also taught at Nizamiyyah in Nishapur for a short time before going back to his hometown of Tabran. He established a small seminary there where he taught and directed students and continued to write.

The Death of Imam Ghazali

Imam Ghazali died on 14th Jumada al-Thani 505 AH (1111 CE) at the age of 53. His younger brother, Imam Ahmad Ghazali, gives an account of his last moments:

'On Monday morning Imam Ghazali woke up, he performed his ritual ablution (*wudu'*) and prayed the predawn prayer (*salat al-fajr*) and then asked for his shroud and kissing it said, "I eagerly accept my Lord's command." He lay down and he was dead.'

May God bless his soul.

The Books of Imam Ghazali

Imam Ghazali was a prolific writer: the Indian historian Shibli Nu'mani has compiled an alphabetical list of all his treatises, essays and books, some running up to 40 volumes, and lists 67 works in all. Some of the books are widely published in different languages, while others remain in manuscript form and yet others are not traceable and only their titles are mentioned.

Among the popular books of Imam Ghazali are *Minhaj al-'Abidin* (*Way of the Worshipful*), *Kimiya' al-Sa'adat* (*The Alchemy of Happiness*), *al-Munqidh min al-Dalal* (*Deliverance from Error*) and *Ihya' 'Ulum al-Din* (*Revival of the Religious Sciences*). T. J. Winter, a specialist in Ghazali, writes,

'The *Revival* then is an attempt to universalise the central transformative experience of the author's career. It reflects his conviction that the conventional learning of the age, treating as it did only the more superficial aspects of man's condition, had failed to shake him from pre-occupation with his selfish concerns. The answer as Ghazali had discovered for himself lay only in internalising the formalities of religion through tasting.'

Select Bibliography

Birgivi, Imam Muhammad, *The Path of Muhammad: A Book on Islamic Morals & Ethics*, translated by T. Bayrak. Bloomington: World Wisdom Books, 2005.

Al-Busiri, Imam Sharaf al-Din, *Qasidah Burdah* (Arabic). Yemen: Dar al-Faqihiyah, n.d. Also translated by H. Yusuf as *The Burda: The Poem of the Cloak*, United Kingdom: Sandala, 2002.

Covey, Stephen R., *Seven Habits of Highly Effective People*, New York: Free Press, 1990.

Al-Ghazali, Abu Hamid, *Deliverance from Error: Five Key Texts Including His Spiritual Autobiography* Al-Munqidh min Al-Dalal, translated and annotated by R. J. McCarthy, Kentucky: Fons Vitae, 2001.

Al-Ghazali, Abu Hamid, *On Disciplining the Soul and Breaking the Two Desires*, introduced and translated by T. J. Winter, Cambridge: Islamic Texts Society, 1995.

Al-Ghazali, Abu Hamid, *The Ninety-Nine Beautiful Names of God*, translated by D. Burrell and N. Daher, Cambridge: Islamic Texts Society, 1992.

Haykal, Muhammad, *The Life of Muhammad*, translated by I. R. al-Faruqi, Kuala Lumpur: Islamic Book Service, 2002.

Khan, Ahmad Reza, *Salam*, translated by G. D. Qureshi, Manchester: World Islamic Mission, 1981.

Nu'mani, Shibli, *Al-Ghazali* (Urdu), Pakistan: National Book Foundation, 1979.

Al-Yahsubi, Qadi 'Iyad ibn Musa, *Muhammad, Messenger of Allah: Ash-Shifa of Qadi 'Iyad*, translated by A. A. R. Bewley, Granada: Medinah Press, 1991.

Westen, Drew, *Psychology: Brain, Mind and Culture*, New York: Wiley & Sons, 1998.

Yusuf, Hamza, *Purification of the Heart*, Chicago: Starlatch, 2004.

(The references to Prophetic sayings are taken from the standard collections of Hadith.)